The Royal Air Force

Handbook

The Definitive MoD Guide

ROYAL AIR FORCE

MINISTRY OF DEFENCE

CONWAY

The Royal Air Force Handbook

The Definitive MoD Guide

CONWAY

The front cover main image shows Typhoon T1s of 29(R) Squadron based at RAF Coningsby, © Geoffrey Lee.
The title page image shows a Hercules C-130J of 24 Squadron based at RAF Lyneham.

This Handbook has been produced by the Directorate of Public Relations (RAF), in conjunction with the Defence Procurement Agency, an Executive Agency of the Ministry of Defence.

Whilst every care has been taken in the compilation of this publication to ensure its accuracy, the editorial team and the publisher cannot accept any responsibility for loss occasioned by any person acting or refraining from action as a result of use of any material in this publication. The views expressed are not necessarily those of the MoD. In carrying advertising, the MoD is not endorsing the products or services offered. Neither is it responsible for the delivery of the service in question.

General enquiries about the RAF or its procedures should be addressed to:
DPR(RAF) Publications, RAF Uxbridge, Middlesex, UB10 0RZ. Email: pr.editor@dsl.pipex.com

Specific equipment enquiries should be addressed to:
DPA Press Office, 1c 2120 MoD Abbey Wood Bristol BS34 8JH tel 0117 9130636/0385
email: DPASecPO@dpa.mod.uk and DPASecP02@dpa.mod.uk
Advertising enquiries to: McMillan-Scott plc 10 Savoy Street London WC2E 7HR 378782316

First published in Great Britain in 2006 by Conway, an imprint of Anova Books, 151 Freston Road, London W10 6TH
www.anovabooks.com   Reprinted 2006

ISBN 10: 1 85753 384 4   ISBN 13: 9-780851-779522

Design and layout by Stephen Dent
Printed by WKT Co. Ltd, China

Contents

Tornado GR4 crew
ready to taxy

The Royal Air Force Handbook

Foreword

by the Secretary of State for Defence the Rt Hon Dr John Reid MP

In the 60 years since the end of the Second World War, the world has transformed. International barriers have been removed by global trade, ever more sophisticated global media and cheaper air travel. The security has also changed beyond recognition. Ideological terrorism has grown and today it recognises no international barriers – in recent years we have seen fanatical attacks, among others, on the financial heartland of New York, the streets of Baghdad, the public transport service of London and the diplomatic community of Nairobi.

For the Armed Forces today it is very difficult to plan for where and in what form their services will be required next. In this highly unpredictable security environment, all three forces must be ready to deploy at a moment's notice to any number of different places in the world.

The Royal Air Force is undergoing as much change as the British Army and the Royal Navy. Whereas 60 years ago it undertook missions that were very often tactically independent from the other Services, today it undertakes tasks jointly with them. To this end it must be ready to assume a more expeditionary role than it was traditionally expected to perform. On Operation Telic the RAF deployed a full command centre to the Middle East, and made a significant contribution to gaining air superiority over Iraq, which in turn enabled the effective progress of the coalition land operation.

Increasingly military operations require the deployment of small expeditionary forces into trouble-spots, together with the right kit and supplies, and a robust logistics infrastructure. The RAF's C-17 and C-130 aircraft, capable of providing strategic and tactical airlift over considerable distances, are increasingly vital to this. For example, our C-17s most recently transported helicopters to Pakistan to provide life saving assistance following the earthquake in Pakistan.

Another feature of military interoperability today is the provision of air support to international forces, 24 hours per day and in all weathers. Recently I visited the six Harrier jets based in Kandahar, Afghanistan, which continue to provide close support to the coalition forces operating there.

In all its roles the RAF is ever more flexible and more accurate. Indeed it is often cited that in the 1991 Gulf War it took four aircraft to strike one target, but on Operation Telic in 2003 it took one aircraft to strike four targets. This notable improvement is the result of an increased defence budget, and our investment in battle-winning technology.

Central to this is the Typhoon jet, which is now in service. Equipped with a new generation of air-to-air and air-to-ground weapons, it represents the cornerstone of UK air power, providing the RAF with a world-leading multi-role capability.

Important as equipment is, today's fast-moving strategic environment requires the Armed Forces to recruit the most able people. The RAF appears to be succeeding in that – I never cease to be impressed by the commitment and professionalism of the servicemen and women who operate, support and maintain the equipment. Without them it would amount to nothing.

Rt. Hon. John Reid MP,
Secretary of State for Defence
December 2005

by Air Chief Marshal Sir Jock Stirrup Chief of Air Staff

It is now just over 100 years since Orville and Wilbur Wright ushered in the age of manned powered flight – an age that has transformed the world in so many ways. It was clear from the earliest days that aviation would have significant military applications. Bleriot's success in crossing the Channel raised as much alarm in Great Britain as it did enthusiasm, and gave force to Lord Northcliffe's "Wake up, England" campaign. And although the First World War was not the beginning of military aviation, the conflict had a dramatic effect on aircraft development. After a little more than a month of war, air power had been instrumental in determining the outcome of two crucial battles: Tannenberg and the Marne. Most significantly, the lessons of that conflict led to the creation of the Royal Air Force itself.

The rationale for an independent Air Force has been reinforced over the years since 1918. The Battle of Britain was a seminal moment for the United Kingdom; one of those rare occasions when the whole course of history was at hazard. Our success in that battle depended on the effective combination of many elements, such as technology, doctrine, training, com-

mand and control – what today we would call lines of development – in the context of the exercise of military power in the third dimension. The 'Dowding System' – an interestingly early example of the Network Enabled Capability so much in our minds today – was

fundamental to victory in 1940, but was the result of years of professional thought about the use of air power allied to technological opportunity.

The principles that lie at the heart of air power have remained largely unchanged. But over the years we have found new ways to use those principles, and new means of giving them even greater effect. Precision bombing, for example, has long been an aspiration of air forces, but only in the last couple of decades has it become a reality. Technology increasingly presents us with opportunities for building on the traditional air power strengths of speed, reach and flexibility; at the same time, it offers ways of reducing or eliminating shortcomings such as lack of persistence. But technology on its own does not provide military capability. If we have had a fault in the past, it has rarely been an unwillingness to embrace new technology; rather, it has been a tendency to try to force that technology into an old doctrinal mould, thus squandering many of the potential benefits. So a professional cadre that can think deeply about air power issues and draw together the many lines of development in a coherent way remains as crucial to the Joint operations of the 21st century as it was to the World Wars of the 20th century. The Royal Air Force is one of the pre-eminent global organisations in this regard. Proud of its heritage, it is at the same time modern, flexible and innovative.

The early decades of military aviation were characterised by the search for ever greater speed, range, altitude and manoeuvrability. The closing years of the 20th century saw the pursuit of precision and survivability. All of these characteristics were of course reflected in

the development of aircraft and weapon systems: the Spitfire, the Lancaster, the jet engine, the air-to-air missile, precision-guided bombs, and stealth – to name but a few. But the challenges of today call for different responses. The uncertainty surrounding the environments in which we may have to operate and the threats we might face drive the need for increased adaptability in our systems. And unpredictable and fluid operational environments place a premium on the rapid availability of accurate information. So adaptability and speed of information will increasingly become critical features of our future systems: hence our focus on Network Enabled Capability.

Network Enabled Capability is about joining together sensors, decision makers and weapon systems in a way that enables us to translate information into rapid and precise military effect. It is not immediately apparent when looking just at major equipments such as air-

craft; it lies in the less obvious realm of digital connections and information processing. But it is coming to underpin the adaptable and rapidly employable capabilities that we need now and in the years ahead. And, as ever, this technological opportunity will need to be matched in the areas of doctrine, training, and command and control.

This handbook details current and future Royal Air Force equipment, and reflects the trends and priorities that I have outlined. It reflects the fact that we, perhaps more than any other Service, rely upon technology to give us our combat edge. But that is only part of the story. The men and women who operate and support the equipment, who develop the intellectual basis for its effective use, and who draw together the many diverse elements to transform it into battle-winning capabilities remain our most important resource. It is they who will realise the potential represented in the weapon systems described in this handbook, and who will truly shape the future of military aviation.

Air Chief Marshal Sir Jock Stirrup
GCB AFC ADC DSc FRAeS FCMI RAF

Information and Web links

The RAF's Vision is to provide an agile and adaptable air force that is able to provide a winning air power contribution to joint operations in support of the UK's Defence Mission. This Handbook represents the present and future planned order of battle of the Royal Air Force, together with some of the elements that play a vital part in the provision of that winning air power in many locations around the world.

Information contained in the book has been drawn from many sources in the Ministry of Defence, including RAF units and squadrons and Strike Command, Personnel & Training Command and Joint Helicopter Command Headquarters staffs. Significant input has also been supplied by the Integrated Project Teams across the Defence Procurement Agency (DPA), the Defence Logistics Organisation (DLO) and the Directorate Capability Resources and Scrutiny in the MoD Central Equipment Capability organisation.

The latest news covering RAF activities and decisions and developments on major equipment programmes can be found on the following websites:

www.raf.mod.uk

www.mod.uk

www.dpa.mod.uk

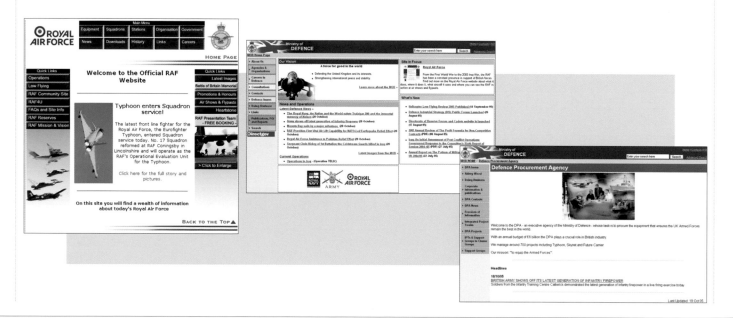

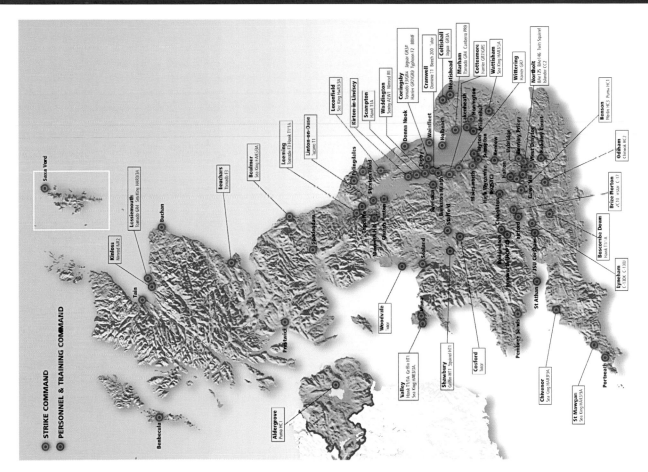

The RAF Mission

To support the Defence Vision, the RAF must be a flexible and agile Air Force that can adapt to new threats and environments; our mission is to:

Produce a battle-winning agile air force: fit for the challenges of today; ready for the tasks of tomorrow; capable of building for the future; working within Defence to achieve shared purpose.

The RAF Vision
The RAF will build upon the successes of the past and on the characteristics that make air power essential across the full spectrum of operations. The RAF's people and their professionalism, dedication and courage will be at the heart of this; they will be trained and enabled to exploit technology to achieve our vision of:

An AGILE and ADAPTABLE Air Force that, person for person, is second to none, and that is able to provide a WINNING air power contribution to joint operations in support of the Defence Mission.

AGILE means our ability to create rapid effect across the full spectrum of operations in a range of environments and circumstances.

ADAPTABLE means our ability to react in an appropriate timescale to new challenges and to seize new opportunities.

Griffin HAR2 on fire-fighting duties in Cyprus

Hercules C-130J taxying at RAF Lyneham

WINNING means success: achieving the end-state through the application of effort, capability and power.

This demands that the RAF should:

Be trained and equipped to deliver air power as a vital contribution to the security of the United Kingdom and as a force for good in the world.

Be modern and flexible, and proud of its heritage

Foster professionalism and team spirit founded

Tornado GR4 and F3 on a low-level sortie

© Paul Bunch

on good leadership, commitment and self-discipline.

Offer opportunity to all, a rewarding and enjoyable career and skills for life.

To achieve these aspirations the RAF has two key objectives:

To recruit, train, lead and motivate its personnel.

To operate effectively at home and abroad as a single Service, or as an element of Joint and Combined operations. ■

Nimrod MR2 deployed in the Gulf region

The Griffin HT1 advanced training helicopter

AIR COMBAT

Harrier GR7 carrying a Maverick on the port mid-wing pylon

1 GROUP

1 Group's Mission is 'To generate and develop effective Combat Air Power'

Number 1 Group Headquarters is the coordinating organization for all front line, Fast-jet Force Elements and as such has functional responsibility for the teeth arm of the Royal Air Force today. Whether it is homeland defence of the UK airspace utilising the Tornado F3, operational flying in Iraq or Afghanistan in the Tornado GR4 and Harrier GR7, or exercising with our NATO partners using the Jaguar GR3A, the unified focus of the 12,000 personnel within Number 1 Group, based across 8 flying stations and one support unit, is being ready for operations, and when called upon providing the battle-winning edge. To do this we must exploit the equipment we have in service now, spreading best practice and evolving our tactics, training and procedures to stay one step ahead in an uncertain world. Be that through home-based training, or exercising in Europe, the Middle East and the United States, we aim to train as we fight in as realistic a way as possible but cognisant of the impact we have on the communities in which we live and work. Through greater use of precision weapons, we will create the desired effect against any potential adversary, exemplified by our performance on Operation Telic in Iraq, where Number 1 Group aircraft were key in shaping the battlespace for a successful Joint and Combined Campaign. Moreover, as we

A four-ship of Jaguar GR3s at high altitude

look forward to working in a Network Enabled environment, where shared situational awareness will allow us to truly practice Effects Based Operations at every level of command, we will embrace the arrival of new systems such as the excellent multi-role Typhoon.

Similarly, by building on the success of the Joint Force Harrier, where Royal Air Force and Royal Naval personnel have worked alongside each other to maximise the effect of the Harrier GR7 and FA2, we will develop a Joint Combat Aircraft capability for land and carrier-borne operations. In all that we do, now and in the future, we will continue to play a major part in an Air Force that strives to be first, and person for person is second to none. ■

Powerplant
Two RB199 turbofans
Thrust: 16,000lbs each

Dimensions
Length: 16.72m
Width: 8.6m
(extended): 13.91m
Weight: 28 tonnes
AAR: Yes
Speed: Mach 1.3
Ceiling: 50,000ft

Aircrew: two

Weapons Systems
Missiles: Storm Shadow
Brimstone
ALARM
AIM-9L
Bombs: Paveway II or III
EPW II or III
BL 755
General Purpose
Gun: Mauser 27mm

Sensors
Radar: Ground Mapping
Targeting: TIALD
LRMTS
Reconnaissance: RAPTOR
DJRP

The Tornado GR4 is a variable-geometry, two-seat, day or night, all-weather attack aircraft, capable of delivering a wide variety of weapons. Powered by two Rolls-Royce RB 199 Mk 103 turbofan engines, the GR4 is capable of low-level supersonic flight and can sustain a high subsonic cruise speed. The aircraft can fly automatically at low level using terrain-following radar when poor weather prevents visual flight. The aircraft is also equipped with forward-looking infrared and is night-vision goggle compatible, making it a capable platform for passive night operations. For navigation purposes, the Tornado is equipped with an integrated global positioning inertial navigation system that can also be updated with visual or radar inputs. The GR4 is also equipped with a Laser Ranger and Marked Target Seeker system that can be used for ground designation or can provide accurate range information on ground targets.

The GR4 can carry up to three Paveway II, two Paveway III or Enhanced Paveway Laser and Global Positioning System Guided Bombs (LGBs), and by using a Thermal Imaging Airborne Laser Designation (TIALD) pod it is able to self-designate targets for LGB delivery. The GR4 also has a ground-mapping radar to identify targets for the delivery of conventional 1000lb bombs and BL755 cluster bombs. All GR4 aircraft are capable of carrying the Air Launched Anti-Radiation Missile (ALARM), which homes on the emitted radiation of enemy radar systems and can be used for the suppression of enemy air defences. The GR4 is capable of carrying up to nine ALARM missiles or a mixed configuration of ALARM missiles and bombs. In the reconnaissance role the GR4 can carry the Digital Joint Reconnaissance Pod to provide detailed reconnaissance imagery; this is currently being replaced with the RAPTOR pod, which provides an even greater day-and-night reconnaissance potential.

For self-protection, the GR4 is normally armed with two AIM-9L Sidewinder short-range air-to-air missiles, a BOZ-107 Pod on the right wing to dispense chaff and flares and a Sky Shadow-2 electronic countermeasures pod on the left wing. The aircraft can also carry an integral 27mm Mauser cannon capable of firing 1700 rounds per minute.

The Tornado GR4 is now equipped with the Storm Shadow missile and will soon be equipped with the new Brimstone missile. The Storm Shadow will allow the Tornado to make precision strikes in poor weather with a greatly increased stand-off range from the target area. Brimstone will provide the Tornado with an effective anti-armour weapon, also providing an enhanced stand-off range.

Tornado GR4 port profile

Tornado GR4 of XV(R) Sqn based at RAF Lossiemouth

The Tornado GR4 is currently operated from two bases. Based at RAF Lossiemouth, in Scotland, are the Operational Conversion Unit, No. 15(R) Squadron, and Nos 12(B), 14 and 617 Squadrons. RAF Marham is the home of the GR4s of Nos II(AC), IX(B), 13 and 31 Squadrons.

In addition to its long-range, high-speed precision strike capability, including supersonic at low level with a low-level combat radius of 400nmls, the Tornado GR4 is a world leader in the specialised field of all-weather, day and night tactical reconnaissance. The new RAP-TOR (Reconnaissance Airborne Pod TORnado) pod is one of the most advanced reconnaissance sensors in the world and greatly increased the effectiveness of the aircraft in the reconnaissance role. Its introduction into service gave the GR4 the ability to download real-time, long-range, oblique-photography data to ground stations or to the cockpit during a mission. The stand-off range of the sensors also allows the aircraft to remain outside heavily defended areas, thus minimising the aircraft's exposure to enemy air-defence systems.

Some Tornado GR4s involved in Operation Telic were fitted with the RAPTOR pod and the aircraft is currently employed in the Gulf on both Close Support and Reconnaissance missions in support of Coalition Forces in Iraq. ■

Powerplant

	RR Pegasus 105 or 107 turbofan
Thrust:	21750lbs (GR7)
	23800lbs (GR7A)
AAR:	Yes
Speed:	660 mph
Ceiling:	43,000ft
Aircrew:	one

Dimensions

Length:	14.36m
Width:	9.25m
Weight:	14 tonnes

Weapons Systems

Missiles:	AIM-9L
	Maverick
Bombs:	Paveway II or III
	EPW II or III
	BL755
	General Purpose
Rockets:	CRV-7 pods

Sensors

Radar:	None
Targeting:	ARBS
	TIALD
Reconnaissance:	DJRP

The Harrier is used by the RAF in the close air support role and is the latest in a long line of 'jump-jets' dating back to the introduction of the first Harriers in the 1960s.

Now, as part of the Joint Force Harrier, these extremely versatile aircraft are ready to deploy anywhere in the world, either on board Royal Navy aircraft carriers or to shore bases.

The aircraft are usually employed in direct support of ground troops tackling such targets as enemy troop positions, tanks and artillery. The Harrier uses a variety of weapons such as Paveway Laser and Global Positioning System-guided bombs against buildings, Maverick infrared missiles against tanks, cluster munitions and general purpose free-fall bombs.

When required, the Harrier can also be equipped with a pod fitted with cameras to provide reconnaissance of the target and battle areas.

For self-defence the aircraft can be fitted with the AIM-9L Sidewinder infrared guided missile.

The first Harriers entered RAF service in 1969, making the RAF the first in the world to use its revolutionary vertical take-off and landing abilities, which allow the aircraft to fly in and out of areas close to the battlefield that would normally be off-limits to conventional aircraft such as the Tornado.

The existing versions of Harrier are the pilot-only GR7 and the two-seat T10 which, when not used as a training aircraft, can also be used in combat. The GR7A has been fitted with a more powerful engine. Key improvements introduced with the GR7 included forward-looking infrared systems, which when used with pilot's night-vision goggles, provide the capability for night-time operations. The aircraft is largely constructed of composite materials and can carry twice the ordnance load of the early model Harriers it succeeded in service.

Since 2000, the RAF's Harriers and the Royal Navy Sea Harriers have been under the organisational control of Joint Force Harrier. This has seen the RAF's aircraft deploy alongside the Sea Harriers on board aircraft carriers of the Royal Navy on many routine training deployments as well as operations. These aircraft are being upgraded to the advanced GR9 standard. ∎

Harrier GR7A port profile

Harrier GR7 on the pre-flight ramp

Powerplant

	RR Pegasus 105 or 107 turbofan
Thrust:	21750lbs (GR9)
	23800lbs (GR9A)
AAR:	Yes
Speed:	660 mph
Ceiling:	43,000ft
Aircrew:	one

Dimensions

Length:	14.36m
Width:	9.25m
Weight:	14 tonnes

Weapons Systems

Missiles:	AIM-9L
	Maverick
Bombs:	Paveway II or III
	EPW II or III
	BL 755
	General Purpose
Rockets:	CRV-7 pods

Sensors

Radar:	None
Targeting:	ARBS
	TIALD
Reconnaissance:	DJRP

The Harrier GR9 is a heavily updated development of the existing GR7, incorporating the ability to use a wide range of advanced precision weaponry, new communications, and systems and airframe upgrades.

Integration and clearance of these weapons will allow the RAF to hit a wider range of targets harder, at longer range and with less risk to aircrew. The first improved aircraft are expected to enter service in 2006 and they will equip Joint Force Harrier squadrons that will be crewed by both Royal Air Force and Royal Navy personnel, following the withdrawal from service of Royal Navy Sea Harrier aircraft.

MoD plans a force of four front-line squadrons and one Operational Conversion Unit. The RAF is expected to supply air and ground crew for two of the front-line squadrons and the RN for the other two while the OCU will be jointly crewed.

Alongside the GR9 upgrade programme, some aircraft are being fitted with more powerful engines to enable them to perform better in extremely hot climates, which degrade the performance of the existing Pegasus Mk105 turbofan. Aircraft with the improved engine

Harrier GR9 ready for take off

© Paul Bunch

will be designated GR9A.

Total projected MoD expenditure on Harrier upgrades, which will be fully realised when the fleet of about 70 aircraft is at GR9 standard, is about £500 million.

Under a £100 million contract awarded to BAE Systems in 2004, new digital weapons that will be integrated onto the GR9 will include the advanced Global Positioning System and laser-guided Paveway IV bomb, and infrared and television variants of the Maverick missile to achieve high precision ground attack capabilities. The aircraft will be able to carry up to six Paveway IV bombs, which will be linked by a new onboard computer.

The Successor Identification Friend or Foe system will also equip the aircraft, to make it less vulnerable on operations.

The aircraft is also expected to be fitted to carry the advanced Brimstone fire and forget anti-armour missile.

Part of the longer term plans for the aircraft currently include equipping with secure communications, a ground proximity warning system and – for training – the Rangeless Airborne Instrumentation and Debriefing System (RAIDS).

The programme also includes an upgrade to the two-seater T10 training aircraft to T12, the equivalent of the GR9 standard. ∎

Head-on view of Harrier GR9.
Note the distinctive anhedral of the
wing surfaces.

© Paul Bunch

Jaguar GR3/GR3A

Powerplant
Two RR Adour turbofans
Thrust: 8249lbs each
AAR: Yes
Speed: Mach 1.4
Ceiling: 40,000 feet

Aircrew: one

Dimensions
Length: 16.83m
Width: 8.69m
Weight: 15.7 tonnes

Weapons Systems
Missiles: AIM-9L/M
Bombs: Paveway II or III
General Purpose
Rockets: CRV-7 pods
Gun: Two 30mm Aden

Sensors
Radar: None
Targeting: LRMTS
Reconnaissance: DJRP

This ground-attack aircraft was the result of a major UK/France collaborative programme, which followed agreement of a joint Anglo-French requirement in 1965 for a dual-role advanced/operational trainer and tactical support aircraft.

The UK ordered about 200 of the aircraft, a mix of single-seat ground-attack aircraft and two-seat trainers of which some 46 remain in first-line service. Deliveries began in 1973, and at its peak the Jaguar equipped eight front-line RAF squadrons in the UK and Germany.

Over the years, the Jaguar has been upgraded to ensure it remains a potent fighter-bomber, and one that served with distinction during the 1991 Gulf War and subsequent operations over Iraq and the Balkans.

The most recent upgrade to GR3A (or T4 for the 2-seat version) standard included improved avionics with the Global Positioning System (GPS) and Terrain-Referenced Navigation (TRN), Night-Vision Goggles (NVG) compatible lighting (both internally and externally), helmet-mounted sight, and new Head-Up and Head-Down Displays in the cockpit. GR3A upgrade also includes a planned ASRAAM capability. These modifications have ensured that the Jaguar is fully capable for performing day and night operations.

The aircraft's twin Adour turbofan engines have also been updated to the Mk106 standard, giving greater fuel economy and more power in high ambient temperatures.

In the reconnaissance role, the Jaguar is fitted with an externally mounted pod, equipped with video-tape and sensors. It can also carry the Thermal Imaging Airborne Laser Designation (TIALD) pod for self-designation of targets or co-operative designation for attacks by other aircraft equipped with precision-guided weapons.

All three front-line squadrons are capable of ground attack and reconnaissance operations, but 41 Sqn is primarily a reconnaissance squadron. The Jaguar force is being run down as Typhoon aircraft start to enter service with the RAF. 54(F) Squadron was disbanded in 2005 and the final Jaguar squadron is planned to disband in 2007. ■

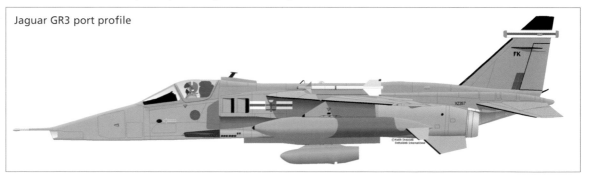

Jaguar GR3 port profile

Jaguar GR3 at medium level

Typhoon F2 — High performance multi-role fighter

Powerplant
2 Eurojet EJ200 turbofans
Thrust: 21,000lbs each
AAR: Yes
Speed: Mach 2
Ceiling: 65,000ft

Aircrew: one

Dimensions
Length: 15.96m
Width: 10.95m
Weight: 21 tonnes

Planned Weapons Systems
Missiles: AMRAAM
ASRAAM
Brimstone
Storm Shadow
Meteor
Bombs: EPW II & III
Paveway IV

Sensors
Radar: Captor ECR90
Pirate IR Search & Track
Targeting: Litening Pod
Reconnaissance: None

Typhoon will provide the RAF with a multi-role combat aircraft, capable of being deployed in the full spectrum of air operations, from air policing, to peace support, through to high intensity conflict.

Britain, Germany, Italy and Spain formally agreed to start development of the aircraft in 1988 with contracts for a first batch of 148 aircraft – of which 55 are for the RAF – signed ten years later. Deliveries to the RAF started in 2003 to 17(R) Sqn, based at BAE Systems Warton Aerodrome in Lancashire, alongside the factory in which the aircraft are assembled, while detailed development and testing of the aircraft was carried out. Formal activation of the Typhoon Squadron at RAF Coningsby occurred on the 1st Jul 2005, with operational employment expected to be declared later on this decade. An incremental acquisition has always been envisaged resulting in a true multi-role weapon system.

Initial production aircraft of the F2 standard will be deployed primarily as air-superiority fighters, but will quickly be equipped with a potent precision ground-attack capability. Armament will include the long-range Advanced Medium Range Air-to-Air Missile (AMRAAM), the UK-developed Advanced Short Range Air-to-Air Missile (ASRAAM) and various air-to-ground weapons. They will succeed in service the RAF's Tornado F3 and Jaguar aircraft.

Following the 55 Tranche 1 aircraft, the RAF is due to receive 89 Tranche 2 aircraft with capacity to be upgraded to deliver further enhanced ground-attack capability and the Meteor Beyond Visual Range Air-to-Air

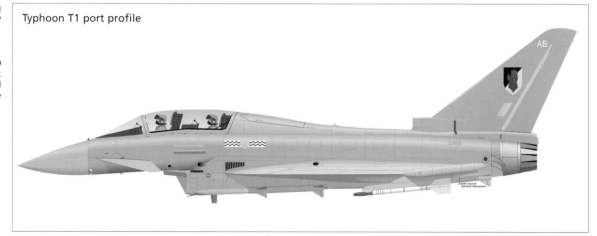

Typhoon T1 port profile

Typhoon F2 demonstrating its agility

Missile. Earlier Tranche 1 aircraft will be upgraded to this standard.

Negotiations were concluded in late 2004 on a contract for the Tranche 2 batch and the placing of a £4.3 billion contract for 89 aircraft was announced that December. Commitment to Tranche 3 procurement is not expected for some years. The MoD is planning for the introduction of multi-role Tranche 2 aircraft with improved ground-attack capabilities, introduced under a planned upgrade programme, to enter service early in the next decade.

This highly capable and extremely agile aircraft is powered by twin turbofans to Mach 2 at 65,000ft. The airframe is largely constructed of carbon fibre composites and light alloys to save weight while the aircraft is equipped with the advanced ECR90 radar, which can track multiple targets at long range. The pilot can carry out many functions by voice command while aircraft manoeuvre; weapon and defensive aid deployment is done through a combined stick and throttle. All of these innovations dramatically simplify operation of the aircraft in combat. Combined with an advanced cockpit that is fully compatible with night-vision goggles, the pilot is superbly equipped for air combat. ■

The state-of-the-art cockpit features voice activated controls

Powerplant
Two RB199 turbofans
Thrust:	16410lbs each
AAR:	Yes
Speed:	Mach 2.2
Ceiling:	50,000ft plus
Aircrew:	two

Dimensions
Length:	18.62m
Width:	8.6m
(extended):	13.91m
Weight:	28 tonnes

Weapons Systems
Missiles:	AMRAAM
	ASRAAM
	Skyflash
	AIM-9L
	ALARM

Sensors
Radar:	Foxhunter AI24
Targeting:	JTIDS
Reconnaissance:	None

he Tornado F3 was selected for development from the original Tornado GR1 attack aircraft in the late 1970s as the RAF's dedicated fighter following an MoD review of other NATO candidate aircraft. A total of 170 were ordered.

The main visible difference from the GR1 or GR4 attack aircraft is the longer fuselage, which permits greater internal fuel stowage.

It entered service at an interim F2 standard with the RAF in 1985. A year later, initial deliveries of the definitive Tornado F3 were made.

Fitted with the long range Foxhunter radar and more powerful engines, the aircraft successively replaced Lightning and Phantom fighter squadrons in the air defence role. Seven squadrons were formed, two of which were subsequently disbanded in view of the reduced threat of air attack to the UK. The variant is also in service with the Royal Saudi Air Force and until the end of 2004 the Italian Air Force leased Tornado F3 aircraft from the RAF.

The pilot in the front seat flies and fights the aircraft, while the rear seat weapons systems officer controls the radar and defensive countermeasures systems.

Two Tornado F3s in their element; at high altitude and with a mixed air-to-air load

Tornado F3 port profile

Tornado F3 is designed to loiter on extended patrol at long range

An important feature of the F3 is its ability to patrol at long distance from its base, supported by air-to-air refuelling.

The aircraft is capable of operation in all weathers and at night, using night-vision goggles.

In the months before the 2003 Gulf War, a small number of Tornado F3s underwent a modification programme to allow them to operate in the Suppression of Enemy Air Defences (SEAD) role. The modifications permitted the carriage of a pair of ALARM missiles in place of the Skyflash or AMRAAM missiles, but the modified aircraft were not in the event deployed during the conflict.

In its usual air defence role, the F3 can receive real-time information on approaching targets through a datalink from patrolling Airborne Early Warning Sentry aircraft and attack nominated targets using AMRAAM missiles. In the anti-radar role, F3s can pass information on the location of an opponent's radar site back to the Sentry or ground-stations for onward relay to other aircraft or ground forces.

Under the AMRAAM Optimisation Programme, these aircraft are being modified to engage several targets simultaneously with greater accuracy and a higher probability of success. ■

Powerplant

P&W F-135 turbofan	
Thrust:	37000 lbs
AAR:	Yes
Speed:	Mach 1.8
Ceiling:	50,000ft plus
Aircrew:	one

Dimensions

Length:	15.52m
Width:	10.67m
Weight:	22.7 tonnes

Weapons Systems

To be decided but expected to include:

Missiles:	AMRAAM
	ASRAAM
Bombs:	Paveway IV

Sensors

Radar:	Active Electronically Scanned Array (AESA)
Targeting:	Integrated into mission system
Recce:	Internal/Pod

The Joint Strike Fighter, which is being built by Lockheed Martin as the F35, will be known in UK service as the Joint Combat Aircraft (JCA) and is planned to replace the RAF and RN's Harriers. Although Lockheed Martin is the prime contractor, the UK is a Level 1 partner with the US and a number of British companies, including BAE Systems and Rolls-Royce, will have extensive involvement in building and developing the aircraft. The UK version will be a multi-role fighter/attack aircraft designed to operate as a STOVL aircraft from land bases and from the next generation of aircraft carriers under study for the RN. This will give the UK a world-beating land-based and sea-based joint expeditionary air power capability well into the middle of the century. When the JCA enters service, it will be able to operate in all weathers, by day and by

JCA demonstrating its short take-off ability

night, for defence of the fleet and for the offensive air support of ground forces. This support will range from close air support to long-range interdiction, as well as anti-surface warfare and tactical reconnaissance. The aircraft will offer several advantages over the Harrier: supersonic flight, improved survivability, internal and external weapons carriage, an increased range and easier supply and maintenance.

The JCA design applies stealth technology techniques and, to minimise its radar signature, the airframe has identical sweep angles for the leading and trailing edges of the wing and tail, and incorporates sloping sides for the fuselage and the canopy. As a further signature-reduction measure, the seam of the canopy and the weapon-bay doors are saw-toothed and the vertical tails are canted at an angle. To achieve the smallest signature possible the aircraft will have the ability to carry a range of weapons internally, rather than carried underneath the aircraft as in current fighters.

The main radar system will be a

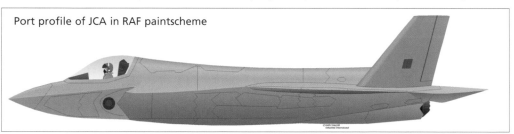

Port profile of JCA in RAF paintscheme

newly developed, electronically scanned array multi-function radar with synthetic aperture capabilities. Targeting information will be supplied by an electro-optical system, which will provide long-range detection and precision targeting by employing thermal imaging, laser tracking and marking, and a forward-looking infrared system. The aircraft's systems will also provide navigation, missile warning and infrared search and track capability.

Early production aircraft will be powered by a Pratt and Whitney F-135 turbofan engine, but there are plans for subsequent aircraft to be offered with a choice of an interchangeable F-136 engine being developed by the General Electric / Rolls Royce Fighter Engine Team. Vertical lift and hover will be achieved by means of a Rolls-Royce developed lift-fan system. Doors installed above and below the vertical fan open as the fan powers up to provide vertical lift. This vertical lift is used in conjunction with the main engine exhaust nozzle at the rear of the aircraft, which swivels down from the horizontal to provide the required lift.

The JCA will place the RAF at the forefront of aviation technology and will give it a multi-role aircraft that will surpass most aircraft or weapons systems in production today, or envisaged in the foreseeable future. Coupled with the Typhoon F2, which is now entering service, it will keep the RAF at the cutting edge of military aviation. ■

JCA hovering over the test facility at Edwards Air Force Base

CASOM/Storm Shadow   Long-range, stand-off, air-to-ground

Dimensions
Length: 5.1m
Wing span: 3m
Weight: 1.3 tonnes

Performance
Speed: Mach 0.8
Range: >130nmls

Aircraft: Tornado GR4
               Typhoon F2

This long-range air-launched and conventionally-armed missile equips RAF Tornado GR4 squadrons and saw operational service in 2003 with 617 Squadron during combat in Iraq, prior to entering full service in 2004. Post deployment analysis demonstrated the missile's exceptional accuracy, and the effect on targets was described as devastating. Based on this performance, it is arguably the most advanced weapon of its kind in the world.

Feasibility studies on a possible UK requirement for a Long Range Stand-Off Missile were originally commissioned in 1982, and work was eventually subsumed in 1986 into the NATO seven-nation Modular Stand-Off Weapon programme. This project proved abortive, and the UK subsequently withdrew. With the end of the Cold War the UK's continued need for a stand-off requirement was reviewed and endorsed as part of the 'Options for Change' exercise. An international competition was

Tornado GR4A with two Storm Shadow fitted on the fuselage pylons

launched in 1994 to meet the UK's Conventionally Armed Stand Off Missile (CASOM) requirement, and seven companies responded.

MBDA (UK)'s Storm Shadow missile was selected, and a development and production contract was awarded in 1997. The French Air Force are also procuring a similar missile, the Scalp EG, from MBDA (France), both weapons being based on the French Apache AP anti-runway missile. The MoD Defence Procurement Agency is also purchasing the Storm Shadow weapon system on behalf of the Italian Air Force.

Storm Shadow is equipped with a powerful UK-developed warhead and is designed to attack important hard-ened targets and infrastructure, such as buried and protected command centres.

Mission data, including target details, is loaded into the weapon's main computer before the aircraft leaves on its mission. After release, the wings deploy and the weapon navigates its way to the target at low level using terrain profile matching and an integrated Global Positioning System.

On final approach to the target the missile climbs, discards its nose cone and uses an advanced infrared seeker to match the target area with stored imagery. This process is repeated as the missile dives onto the target, using higher-resolution imagery, to ensure the maximum accuracy. ■

Storm Shadow

This weapon was procured for RAF Harrier GR7 aircraft following analysis of air operations over Kosovo in 1999, when cloud cover and poor weather limited the effectiveness of RAF strikes.

MoD contracted with the Raytheon Corporation in 2000 to integrate the weapon onto the Harrier and it entered service with the RAF early the following year.

Maverick is in use with the air forces of 27 countries and has a proven track record of operational success. The weapon was successfully used by the RAF during operations in Iraq in 2003.

The weapon is designed for close air support and defence suppression and can be used against armour, ships and transport and fuel-storage facilities. The G2 version, with which the RAF is equipped, has an Imaging

Two Mavericks with protective sensor caps

Weight:	0.28 tonnes
Length:	2.59m
Range:	6.5nmls
Seeker:	Imaging Infrared
Aircraft:	Harrier GR7

Infrared (IIR) seeker which gives the weapon a true all weather, day or night 'fire-and-forget' capability against armoured and mobile targets.

It locks on to its target before launch, at low or medium level, and flies to the target. The weapon has a maximum range of 12 kilometres, which helps the launch aircraft to minimise its exposure to hostile air defence weapons.

The weapon sends a 'picture' of the heat-generated image of the target from its IIR seeker head to a Multi-Purpose Colour Display (MPCD) in the GR7's cockpit. The pilot identifies the target, locks the missile onto it and fires the missile once the target is in range. The Maverick will then home onto the target while the delivery aircraft carries out escape manoeuvres. ■

Maverick AGM

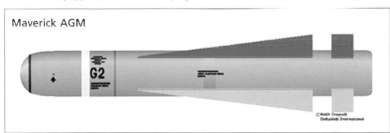

Brimstone

Weight:	49kg
Length:	1.8m
Width:	0.3m
Range:	<10 nmls
Speed:	Supersonic
Sensor:	Millimetric Wave radar
Aircraft:	Tornado GR4
	Harrier GR9
	Typhoon F2

This advanced radar-guided weapon is derived from the US Army Hellfire AGM-114F missile and is deployed in RAF service on a pylon-mounted launching rack that will contain three missiles.

It is powered by a rocket motor and can seek and destroy targets at long range.

Ground acquisition and target recognition are achieved by a millimetric wave radar seeker. The weapon locks onto a target after launch and is designed for the attack and destruction of armoured targets. Steerable fins guide the missile towards the target with final impact causing a tandem charge warhead to detonate. The first, smaller warhead nullifies reactive armour, allowing the follow-through charge to penetrate the main armour. It is designed to be carried by the Tornado GR4, Harrier

Tornado GR4s carrying a full complement of Brimstone missiles

Brimstone missile

Fully autonomous, fire-and-forget, anti-armour missile

GR9 and Typhoon. The weapon can be used in Indirect and Direct modes. For Indirect attack weapons are launched when the targets and their position are not visible to the attacking aircraft. In Direct mode the pilot can use an on-board sighting system to select the target, which can lie off the aircraft's track, so that pilots do not need to manoeuvre to release weapons. The weapon flies at low level, using its onboard navigation systems to head for the target and searching, using its radar, to distinguish between valid and non-valid targets. Brimstone can be programmed to start searching only in target areas, limiting risks to friendly forces.

MoD wanted a weapon that could operate in all weathers, day and night, be effective against the future predicted Explosive Reactive Armour arrays and be a genuine 'fire-and-forget' weapon.

Brimstone will replace the BL755 cluster bombs in the anti-armour role.

After a strong competition between four rival projects, a contract was let with MBDA in 1996. Total expected cost of introducing the weapon into service is about £850 million.

The weapon went into service on the Tornado GR4 in 2005. Work continues to ensure the weapon reaches its full potential. ■

Three Brimstone missiles sandwiched between two ALARMs

Weight:	0.265 tonnes
Length:	4.30m
Width:	0.244m
Speed:	supersonic
Guidance System:	Passive Radar Homing
Aircraft:	Tornado GR4
	Tornado F3
	Typhoon F2

The Air Launched Anti-Radiation Missile (ALARM) is designed to destroy or suppress the use of enemy ground-based air-defence radar systems.

The BAE Systems weapon was selected ahead of the US High Speed Anti-Radiation Missile (HARM) following a two-way contest for the MoD order during the 1980s.

It first saw service during the Gulf War of 1991 and has been in the weapon inventory of the Tornado ground attack aircraft ever since, including the latest GR4 model.

Combinations of between two and seven missiles can be carried on each aircraft. Since its original entry into service, radars have become increasingly more sophisticated in their ability to avoid detection and attack by anti-radiation weapons such as ALARM; consequently, the missile has been upgraded and the improved capability ALARM has entered service with the RAF's Tornado squadrons.

An armourer fits ALARM missiles

The ALARM operates by homing onto the radar energy being emitted by the target radar in several ways. If the target is active and emitting radiation when the missile is launched, the ALARM will fly direct to the target. If the targeted radar is quiet when the missile is launched, the ALARM will fly to a pre-set point above the target and loiter under a parachute in the area until the radar switches on. It will then eject the parachute and home onto the target. In Area Suppression mode the missile can be fired in the direction of radars whose positions are unknown and it will engage the highest priority target for attack. In Direct mode the missile is pre-programmed with threat radars and executes a box-search for them after launch, homing onto the highest priority target.

The missile can be pre-loaded with a prioritised file of hostile radars, for which it will search after launch.

Some Tornado F3s were modified to carry ALARMs for operations over Iraq during 2003. ∎

ALARM missile

A Tornado GR4 displaying a full load of ALARM missiles

Paveway II & III

Length:	3.68m (PII)
	4.45m (PIII)
Width:	0.42m (PII)
	0.92m (PIII)
Weight:	0.546 tonnes (PII)
	1.141 tonnes (PIII)
Aircraft:	Harrier GR7
	Tornado GR4
	Typhoon F2
	Jaguar GR3

The original version of the Paveway II laser-guided bomb entered service with the RAF in the 1970s and is composed of a standard UK 450kg bomb with a computer control group fitted to the nose, supporting a laser seeker head and steerable fins. A tail unit is fitted with fins that deploy after launch from the aircraft. Laser designation of targets can be provided by the Thermal Imaging Airborne Laser Designation (TIALD) pod, or from troops on the ground using a laser target designator.

The bomb's guidance package takes over on release from the aircraft and steers the bomb on to the source of reflected laser energy. The bomb can be dropped from low or medium level. During the Gulf War of 1991,

Enhanced Paveway

Paveway III LGB

Tornado aircraft dropped weapons on targets designated by Tornados carrying TIALD pods and by Buccaneers carrying the Pave Spike pod. Paveway II equips Tornado GR4, Harrier GR7 and Jaguar GR3 aircraft.

Paveway III is an upgraded LGB and is designed specifically to defeat hardened targets, such as protected underground command posts. When Paveway III is released from an aircraft it flies on a pre-programmed course towards its target, using a flight profile designed to give it the best approach to achieve a successful attack. It carries a 900kg penetrator

warhead that is steered to the target by a more advanced and precise guidance package, compared with that fitted to the smaller Paveway II bomb. Steerable vanes on the front of the bomb are controlled by a proportional guidance system that increases accuracy, and its range by limiting the amount of kinetic energy lost in maneuvering. Computer-controlled shaping of the attack trajectory maximises the bomb's capacity for penetrating a considerable depth of reinforced concrete to destroy a target.

Paveway III equips Tornado GR4 aircraft. ∎

Lessons learned during the 1999 Kosovo conflict identified the need for the RAF to be able to strike static, mobile and armoured targets accurately in all weathers and 24 hours a day.

The Enhanced Paveway (EPW) family of weapons was procured to meet this requirement and the EPWII entered RAF service in 2001 and the larger EPWIII entered service in late 2002. Harrier GR7 can carry the EPWII and both weapons are carried by Tornado GR4.

Both EPWII and EPWIII are based on the laser-guided bombs Paveway II and Paveway III respectively, already in RAF service, and use the same warheads and fin sections.

However, the EPW weapons have a modified guidance section and wiring to accommodate a Global Positioning System Aided Inertial Navigation System (GAINS).

Once released from the launch aircraft, EPW is fully autonomous in cases where there is cloud cover over the target which may obstruct the laser and prevent weapon guidance. In these instances, it is steered to the target using Global Positioning System (GPS) information as well as guidance from its on-board inertial navigation unit.

EPWIII milliseconds before impact on a hard target

Length:	EPWII - 3.68m
	EPWIII - 4.39m
Weight:	EPWII - 545kg
	EPWIII - 1130kg

In good weather, or where rules of engagement are more demanding, aircrews can guide the weapon to the assigned target using the laser guidance contained within both weapons. Laser designation may be provided from the air using a Laser Designator, or from forces on the ground using a laser target designator.

The EPWII includes a 450kg general-purpose warhead; the EPWIII includes the 900kg class penetrator warhead. Both of the EPW variants have demonstrated the same degree of accuracy in their laser mode (without the use of GAINS) as their predecessors, and highly accurate results have been achieved on trials using the GPS autonomous mode. Both LGBs have been well-received by the RAF. These weapons were used during operations in Iraq in 2003. ■

Enhanced Paveway

Length:	3.1m
Weight:	225kg
Guidance:	GPS & INS & Laser
Aircraft:	Harrier GR7
	Tornado GR4
	Typhoon F2

This advanced and highly accurate weapon will provide the RAF's strike fleet with a state-of-the-art precision guided bomb when it enters service in 2007 replacing the existing Paveway II and Enhanced Paveway II weapons and 505kg unguided general purpose bombs. Equipped with the latest Global Positioning Guidance technology, Paveway IV is a low-cost, all-weather, 24-hour precision bombing capability able to defeat the majority of general-purpose targets.

Paveway IV will significantly minimise collateral damage through one of the world's most advanced fuses fitted with a 'Late-Arm' safety device that will not allow an off-course munition to arm. It will also be fitted with a warhead designed to meet the latest requirements of NATO Insensitive Munition safety policy.

The increased accuracy of the system allows for a warhead half the size

Paveway IV LGBs carrying trials markings

(225kg) of conventional Paveway II bombs. Paveway IV's lighter weight provides greater flexibility given the potential for a single aircraft to carry more of the weapons and so strike more targets in a single pass. The weapons can be reprogrammed with target data by the aircrew while airborne.

Other improvements over older weapons include less drag, greater accuracy, higher resistance to jamming, better supportability, zero maintenance, lower cost and a significant improvement in safety through the use of safer explosive compounds. The first platform to receive the weapon will be the Harrier GR9 with Tornado GR4 and Typhoon F2 to follow. Paveway IV is also a candidate weapon for JCA. Warhead trials and tests using an Environmental Test Vehicle variant were under way during 2005. ∎

Paveway IV

General Purpose Bombs Freefall or retarded, unguided

These unguided high explosive bombs have been in the RAF's inventory for decades and their basic designs dates back to those used in the Second World War, adapted for use on supersonic strike aircraft.

General purpose bombs come in two types, the 505kg and a smaller 312kg version. The 505kg bomb forms the basic warhead used in the RAF's existing Paveway II laser guided bomb system, when provided with a laser seeker and guidance vane packages.

The larger of the two weapons can be used by Tornado GR4, Jaguar GR3 and Harrier GR7/9 aircraft. The smaller 312kg is not used by Tornado GR4.

Both the 505kg and the 312kg weapon use unitary blast warheads and both can be dropped as freefall bombs or fitted with a retarder unit, which rapidly slows the bomb in flight, allowing aircraft to drop a bomb at low level over the target and get clear before detonation.

Both weapons have three modes of detonation. They can be preset to detonate above a target in airburst mode to provide the maximum fragmentation effect for attack of unprotected targets.

Another mode is impact detonation, for achievements of maximum blast damage to unprotected targets.

The final mode is post-impact delay, in which the bomb will detonate after a pre-set delay, allowing it to penetrate a target structure. The length of the delay can be varied to achieve the best effects against individual targets. ■

505kg bombs ready to be loaded onto GR7s in the Gulf

Length:	2.18m or 2.48kg
Width:	0.33m or 0.42m
Weight:	312kg or 505kg

Aircraft:	Tornado GR4
	Jaguar GR3
	Harrier GR7

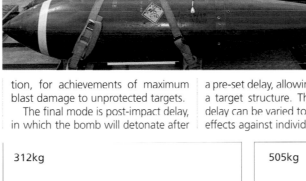

312kg

505kg

Aircraft: Harrier GR7
             Jaguar GR3

This unguided weapon equips Harrier GR7 and Jaguar GR3 and comes in two versions, for attacks on lightly protected installations, ships or armoured forces.

The rocket pod will also equip the Army's force of Apache attack helicopters.

The CRV-7 uses a modular warhead, fitted to a rocket motor and is launched from a streamlined pod, each of which contains 19 rockets.

The weapons are launched in a pre-programmed ripple at targets sighted visually by pilots.

Rockets can be fitted with a high

A Harrier GR7 ripple-fires a salvo of CRV-7 rockets at low level

CRV-7 fired in a shallow dive

explosive, semi-armour piercing warhead for attacks on unarmoured targets and a kinetic energy penetrator, which contains no explosive, for attacks on armoured targets.

The rockets have a high impact speed and can be launched up to three miles from targets. ■

CRV-7 rocket pod

Cluster Bomb Unguided low-level area attack/denial bomblets

The RAF's inventory of cluster bombs are carried and released in a similar manner to other bombs but, when released, the bombs break open in the airflow and release 147 high-explosive bomblets into the target area. This allows multiple targets to be attacked with one weapon, rather than a number of missions with single-warhead weapons. This is of great advantage in a high-threat environment, particularly when the targets are mobile. The BL755 bomb dispenses its bomblets into the airflow shortly after the weapon leaves the aircraft, and on impact with the ground, or a target, the bomblets detonate, producing a high-velocity plasma jet that can penetrate armour up to 250mm thick. In addition, the bomblet casing breaks into shrapnel fragments that are capable of destroying soft-skinned vehicles and equipment. Recent improvements to the bomblets, designated IBL755, include better reliability and armour penetration. Both the BL755 and the IBL755 bombs are delivered from low-level attacks.

RBL755 is a modification of the original BL755 to give the cluster bomb an anti-armour capability from a medium-level attack. A radar-prox-

Cluster bomb

imity, height-detecting sensor in the tail causes the bomblets to be dispensed after the weapon falls to a pre-determined height just above the

target. This release system negates further aircraft involvement, and allows the aircraft to fly at a safer weapon-delivery level.

The BL/IBL/RBL755 cluster bombs are unguided. The bomblets are distributed in an approximately oval shape of some 150 metres by 60 metres around the target. This weapon is planned to be withdrawn from service by the end of 2009. ■

An armourer checks the fastenings on a BL755

Mauser 27mm & Aden 30mm cannon

he Mauser BK-27 is a 27mm cannon fitted to the Tornado F3 and the Tornado GR4 aircraft for air-to-air or air-to-ground firing. The cannon is a single-barrel, high performance, breech-cylinder gun operated by a fully automatic electrically fired gas-operated system at a selective rate of 1000 or 1700 rounds per minute.

The belted-link ammunition box is positioned to the side of the gun-feed mechanism and a floating buffer system imposes a very small recoil and vibration load on the airframe of the aircraft. Spent cartridge cases and empty links are ducted from the rear of the gun into a collection bay immediately behind the gun. Automatic ram air purges the gun compartment and spent cases bay during and after firing.

The weapon has a very good hit-accuracy and one of its main strengths is the cannon's ability to achieve a full 1700-rounds-per-minute rate of fire almost from the first round. This is an important asset, particularly if the cannon is being used against a fast-moving target. Targeting of the cannon is done through the aircraft's head-up-display (HUD). When the cannon is selected in the cockpit, a firing predictor is projected onto the HUD; this depicts a moving line (continuously compacted impact line), or snake, that predicts where the next few rounds of cannon fire will go. The cannon can be aimed by using either a prediction sight or, in the case of the F3, a radar-designated sight.

The cannon has a very high muzzle velocity and its high rate of fire, coupled with its ability to fire several different types of high-explosive shells, make it equally suitable for both interceptor-type aircraft and ground-attack aircraft alike. The system is relatively compact, extremely robust and its simple, rugged design makes it highly reliable.

The Aden cannon is a fully automatic, single-barrelled, five-chambered rotating cylinder gun, which is fitted to the Jaguar GR3 and the Hawk T1A. It is electrically fired and gas operated with a rate of fire of between 1200 and 1400 rounds per minute.

The Jaguar GR3 has two cannon housed in port and starboard gun bays in the lower centre fuselage. The cannon's 30mm ammunition is contained in two boxes mounted in compartments above the gun bays, with each box holding 150 rounds formed into a belt by metal links. During firing, the spent cartridge cases are ejected overboard and the empty links are retained in a compartment inboard and below the gun bays. The guns are harmonised in the aircraft by

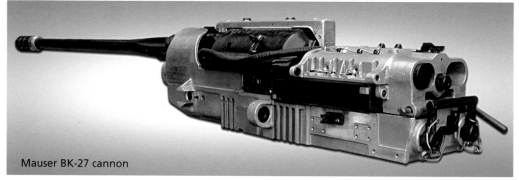

Mauser BK-27 cannon

Aden 30mm cannon

The ventral pack of the Aden cannon is clearly visible on this Hawk T1A

aligning the aircraft on the ground with a pre-positioned sighting board and adjusting the guns onto aligning marks on the board. Aiming of the guns is done through the aircraft's HUD, which depicts a gun-aiming symbol with a centre dot. The aircraft is flown to maintain the centre dot over the marked target cross.

The single Aden cannon operated by the Hawk T1A is housed in an external gun-pod assembly bolted to the underside of the fuselage on the centre-line of the aircraft. The pod contains the cannon and a close-packed ammunition drum containing 100 rounds; it is possible to load a further 30 rounds into the system by using the feed chute. The ammunition ejection sequence follows the same pattern as the system on the Jaguar, with the empty cartridges ejected overboard and the links retained in a compartment at the rear

of the pod. The cannon can be harmonised with the aircraft's HUD to give a firing imagery display, which the pilot aligns onto the target.

The cannon is able to fire ball ammunition or high-explosive-tipped rounds and is used by the Hawk for air-to-air and air-to-ground training and by the Jaguar in the air-to-ground role. The cannon has proved to be a very reliable weapon for many years in both its operational and training roles. ■

M60D Machine Gun & M134 Minigun

Aircraft: Chinook

The M60D machine gun is a 7.62mm calibre automatic, gas-operated machine gun that is mounted on the Chinook helicopter and can be fired from either side of the cabin, or from the aircraft's rear ramp. The gun is attached to a mount fixed to the aircraft that permits it to swivel freely between mechanical stops, which pre-vent damage to the aircraft during fir-ing. An ammunition-can assembly, and an ejection-control bag to collect spent cartridge cases, are supplied to each mount and are fitted directly to the gun. The gun is fired manually at up to 550 rounds per minute.

The M134 Minigun is a 7.62mm air-cooled, percussion-fired, multi-bar-relled rotary gun, which is mounted on the Chinook helicopter. The gun is electrically driven from the aircraft's 115V AC supply and is mounted on either the port or starboard side of the aircraft in the escape hatch or the cabin door respectively. The gun is fired manually, using belt-fed ammunition at up to 4000 rounds per minute. ■

M60D Machine Gun being fired from the rear ramp

Chinook on operations, with starboard cabin door open

M134 Minigun mounted in the starboard door

Air-to-air BVR missile

Length:	3.66m
Wingspan:	0.526m
Diameter:	0.177m
Launch weight:	150kg
Range:	Over 20nmls
Speed:	Mach 2.5+
Guidance system:	Inertial mid-course/Active radar terminal
Aircraft:	Tornado F3 Typhoon F2

The AIM-120B AMRAAM was initially procured for the Royal Navy's Sea Harrier; however, it was subsequently partially integrated onto the Tornado F3 as an enhancement to the aircraft's beyond-visual-range (BVR) capability. Full integration onto the Tornado F3 was completed during 2004. AMRAAM will also equip the Typhoon F2 when it enters RAF service. AMRAAM can be used in all weather conditions and is scheduled to be operational with the RAF into the next decade.

AMRAAM is faster than Skyflash, which it replaces on the F3, and incorporates an active radar with an inertial reference unit and a datalink microcomputer system. This equipment makes the missile less dependent on the fire-control radar of the firing aircraft.

In a typical BVR engagement, the AMRAAM is launched from a range of 20 to 30nmls and is then guided by

Four AMRAAM housed on the main fuselage of the F3

its own inertial navigation system, while receiving command-guidance updates from the launch aircraft via the data link, until it reaches the target area. The missile then enters the final, or terminal phase, where its own monopulse radar detects the target and guides to impact. The missile is equipped with a radar proximity fuse, which detonates the high-explo-sive fragmentation warhead at a preset distance from the target. In short-range mode, the missile can be launched 'active-off-the-rail', when the missile's radar detects the target immediately after launch.

In 2004 MoD placed an £80 million contract with Raytheon Missile Systems for the latest AIM-120 C5 variant. The new missile, which will enter service in 2007, incorporates the latest technology and includes a greater immunity to countermeasures, a better range and a more effective warhead. It will supersede the earlier B model, which is approaching the end of its in-service life. ■

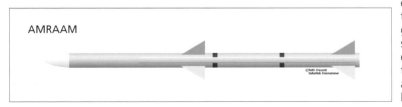

AMRAAM

Tornado F3 carrying two AMRAAM partially recessed into its forward fuselage

Air-to-air IR missile

Length:	2.9m
Diameter:	0.166m
Launch weight:	87kg
Range:	8nmls
Speed:	Mach 3+

Guidance system:
IR staring array with inertial guidance

Aircraft: Tornado F3
Typhoon F2

The AIM-132 ASRAAM is a high speed, highly manoeuvrable, heat-seeking, air-to-air missile. Built by MBDA UK Ltd, the missile is designed as a 'fire-and-forget' weapon, able to counter intermittent target obscuration in cloud as well as sophisticated infrared (IR) counter-measures. Although ASRAAM is pre-dominantly intended for use in the within-visual-range (WVR) arena, it also has capabilities that permit its use in the beyond-visual-range arena.

The missile uses a new Raytheon Imaging IR seeker head and it is the world's first IR missile to enter service using a sapphire-domed staring array detector, which detects the whole target scene. When combined with digital signal-processing and imaging software, ASRAAM is able to see individual areas of its target, such as engines, cockpit or wings. The picture is very similar to a monochrome TV picture, and gives the missile excellent long-range target acquisition, even against employed counter-

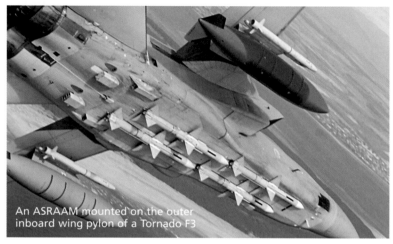

An ASRAAM mounted on the outer inboard wing pylon of a Tornado F3

measures such as flares or similar pyrotechnics. In addition to its ability to image targets, the seeker also allows the missile to be fired at very high off-boresight angles, in either lock-before or lock-after-launch modes. Because the missile has a fire-and-forget capability, the pilot can engage multiple targets with several missiles simultaneously. To increase its speed and its operating range, the missile has a low-drag design; only tail fins are provided for control purposes; and a new, low-signature, dual-burn, high-impulse solid rocket motor provides the power. Compared to other similar missiles, this new motor improves both the missile's instantaneous acceleration and its maximum cruise velocity.

In a typical WVR engagement, the ASRAAM is slaved to the target either visually or by the launch aircraft's on-board sensors. Following release, the missile accelerates to speeds in excess of Mach 3 whilst being guided to the target using its IR seeker. Detonation of the high-explosive fragmentation warhead is achieved by either a laser proximity fuse or an impact fuse. ∎

ASRAAM

©Keith Draycott
DeltaWeb International

The Skyflash is a supersonic, medium-range, air-to-air missile developed by the UK from the American AIM-7 Sparrow missile. The latest version of the missile has a boost-sustain, solid fuel rocket motor giving it a greater range than previous versions. The missile can intercept and destroy enemy targets in all weather conditions, with the ability to 'snap-up' or 'snap-down' to engage targets at ultra-high or low level. The missile discriminates between separate target groups and can operate in a variety of countermeasure environments.

The Skyflash missiles on the F3 are recessed into the underside of the aircraft and are launched by large rams forcing them away from the launch aircraft. The missile uses semi-active homing, where the launch aircraft illuminates the target and the missile uses its built-in radar receiver to home on the reflected energy. This semi-active guidance limits the launch aircraft's ability to manoeuvre until missile impact, as the launch aircraft must maintain positive radar contact with the target. In a typical beyond-visual-range (BVR) engagement the missile is launched and semi-actively guided until the active-radar proximity fuse detonates the high-explosive fragmentation warhead near to the target.

Although Skyflash is primarily a BVR missile, it can also be employed at shorter ranges, where the missile is optimised to ensure quick reaction times and maximum manoeuvrability after it has been launched. ■

Skyflash

The main armament of the Tornado F3 for over 20 years, the Skyflash missile is based on the AIM-7 Sparrow in US service

Air-to-air BVR missile

Length:	3.66m
Wingspan:	1.02m
Diameter:	0.203m
Launch weight:	208kg
Range:	Over 20nmls
Speed:	Mach 2+
Guidance system:	Inertial mid-course/Active radar terminal
Aircraft:	Tornado F3

Air-to-air IR missile

Length:	2.87m
Diameter:	0.13m
Launch weight:	84.28kg
Range:	Over 6nmls
Speed:	Mach 3+
Guidance system:	
	IR reticule seeker

Aircraft:	Tornado GR4
	Harrier GR7
	Jaguar GR3
	Hawk T1A

The Sidewinder AIM-9 is a supersonic, heat-seeking, short range, air-to-air missile capable of being launched from a vast array of aircraft types. The Sidewinder's main components are an infrared (IR) homing guidance section, an active optical target-detector, a high-explosive warhead and a rocket motor. The in-built IR seeker allows the pilot to launch the missile, then leave the area, or take evasive action, while the missile guides itself to impact by homing on the engine exhaust of the target aircraft. IR homing allows the missile to be used by day or by night and in electronic countermeasure conditions. The Sidewinder is the most widely used air-to-air missile in the world and is one of the oldest, least expensive and most successful missiles ever produced.

The Sidewinder has been continually updated over the years and the AIM-9L and AIM-9L/I versions used by the RAF have enhanced guidance characteristics, which give them the

AIM-9 Sidewinders being mounted onto a Tornado GR4

ability to attack targets from all angles, including head-on. Installation of a conical scan-system increased the seeker's sensitivity, improved tracking stability and gave the missile a much-improved resistance to IR decoys.

The Sidewinder is a within-visual-range missile, slaved to the target either manually by the pilot, or by using one of the aircraft's sensors. It is a 'dogfight' missile and so launches

and arms itself very quickly, thus allowing it to be employed at very short range. Once launched, the missile is guided to the target using IR homing and the annular blast-fragmentation warhead is detonated once the target is inside the missile's lethal radius. The Sidewinder is a fire-and-forget missile, allowing the pilot to fire several missiles at different targets within a very short time frame. ∎

AIM-9 Sidewinder

© Keith Draycott
DeltaWeb International

Hawk T1A carrying
Sidewinder missiles

Digital Joint Reconnaissance Pod

Length:	2.81m
Diameter:	1.4m
Weight:	254kg
Aircraft:	Jaguar GR3
	Harrier GR7
	Tornado GR4

The Digital Joint Reconnaissance Pod (DJRP) is mounted on the centre-line pylon of the Jaguar GR3A, the Harrier GR7 and the Tornado GR4 aircraft. The DJRP contains various electronically-scanned sensors, a number of electro-optical camera options and an Infrared Line Scanner (IRLS). All sensors record to analogue SVHS tapes that provide high-resolution still or moving images of the target area to a software-based Ground Imagery Exploitation System. The various EO camera options that can be fitted to the DJRP enable it to be operated either at medium level or at low level. For medium-level operation, one camera is mounted in the nose of the pod

Jaguar GR3 with a DJRP on the centreline pylon

DJRP pod in low-visibility grey

and can be rotated through 180°, from horizon-to-horizon. In the low-level mode, two fixed-depression EO cameras are mounted on either side of the pod, giving left-hand and right-hand coverage of the aircraft's track. The IRLS is common to all camera fits and is mounted in the rear of the pod, where it gives a slightly forward-looking, almost vertical, horizon-to-horizon coverage.

When mounted on the Jaguar GR3A, the pod is designed to be used in a fully-automated mode against known targets, pre-planned on the Jaguar Mission Planner. To achieve a greater measure of mission flexibility, however, the pod can also be manually controlled by the pilot against targets of opportunity. After taking target

images in manual mode, the pod can be switched back to automatic mode to continue with the pre-planned mission. Whilst medium-level operations are conducted by all three front-line Jaguar squadrons, only 41(F) Squadron operates the DJRP in the low-level, tactical reconnaissance role. The Harrier GR7 and the Tornado GR4 operate the pod in manual mode only, in both medium and low-level operations.

The digital capability of the pod could eventually enable it to send real-time, data-burst images to an E-3D Sentry or Nimrod R1 for onward transmission and download by the commander on the battlefield. This will give the commander an almost instant recce picture of an area or target at any given moment. ∎

TIALD is a second-generation laser designator pod, which initially entered service in the 1991 Gulf War when it was used as a laser designator for the bombs carried by Tornado GR1s. The pods are designed to be operable 24-hours a day and comprise a high-resolution FLIR (forward-looking infrared), a laser designator and a tracking system. Most previous designation systems required the pilot or weapon systems officer (WSO) to keep the target tracked manually; however,

TIALD allows automatic tracking once the target is locked. Initially, the TIALD pod is pointed at the target by the aircraft's navigation system; once the pilot or WSO has identified the target on his cockpit display the aiming cross is positioned over the target and the pod is switched into automatic tracking mode. At the appropriate moment during the attack, the TIALD laser is turned on, which provides the bomb's guidance system with the required information to complete the attack.

The whole process is recorded and can be replayed after landing to assess the success of the mission.

The TIALD pod was modified to provide a TV sensor in addition to the infrared sensor and, following a number of other upgrades, the current 400-Series pod is now flown on the Tornado, Harrier and Jaguar ground-attack aircraft. A further upgrade is planned to the pod sensors and electronics, after which it will be re-designated as the 500-Series pod. ■

Specifications

Length:	2.9m
Diameter:	0.3m
Weight:	230kg
Aircraft:	Tornado GR4
	Harrier GR7
	Jaguar GR3

TIALD's movable IR sensor pod

A Jaguar GR3 carries a TIALD pod on the centreline

Specifications

Length:	5.8m (19ft 2ins)
Width:	0.8m (2ft 7ins)
Height:	0.75m (2ft 6ins)
Weight:	1000kg (2200lbs)
Aircraft:	Tornado GR4

Reconnaissance Airborne Pod for Tornado, RAPTOR, which is built by BF Goodrich Aerospace, is a new stand-off electro-optical and infrared (IR), long-range oblique-photography pod fitted to the Tornado GR4. The images received by the pod can be transmitted via a real-time data-link system to image analysts at a ground station, or can be displayed in the cockpit during flight. The imagery can also be recorded for post-flight analysis. The RAPTOR system can create images of hundreds of separate targets in one sortie; it is capable of autonomous operation against pre-planned targets, or it can be re-tasked

RAPTOR pod on a Tornado GR4

manually for targets of opportunity or to select a different route to the target. The stand-off range of the sensors allows the aircraft to remain outside heavily-defended areas, to minimise the aircraft's exposure to enemy air-defence systems.

The RAPTOR pod contains a dual-band (visible and IR) sensor, which is capable of detecting and identifying small targets from either short range or long range and from medium or high altitudes, by day or by night. The optical sensors gather high-resolution, motion-free images of extraordinary detail. The optical images are support-

ed by IR imagery that can reveal differences in the shape, composition or content of objects from their thermal signatures. Daytime IR also offers superior haze-penetration in poor weather conditions, while the night time imagery can reveal details such as the fuel levels in storage tanks. The aircraft weapon systems officer controls the RAPTOR system using a real-time cockpit video display, enabling verification of target acquisition, and the conduct of tasks such as battle-damage assessment, or recording the images on digital tape for further in-depth, post-operation analysis. ■

RAPTOR is fitted to the centreline fuselage hardpoint

RF RADOME NO PUSH

Conway

Incorporating Brassey's and Putnam Aeronautical Books

Pioneering publishing on land, at sea and in the air

Conway publishes a wide range of high-quality reference books for all those interested in maritime, naval, military and aviation history.

Our well-established list of titles includes the famous 'Anatomy of the Ship' monographs, which provide complete information on many individual ships from HMS *Victory* to the battleship *Yamato*. The Conway range also includes the world famous Putnam Aeronautical series detailing the world's aircraft manufacturers, their aircraft and their individual histories. Other popular publications include the respected naval annual *Warship*, the *Model Shipwright* quarterly journal and the *Royal Navy Handbook* (a sister volume to the *Royal Air Force Handbook*).

In addition Conway publishes a wide range of well-researched and superbly presented history books written by the leading writers in their fields. Recent titles include *Winston Churchill: Soldier, The Island Nation, Wars of the Cold War, The Sea Chart* and *The Ships of Trafalgar.*

For more information on all of our titles visit the Conway website at www.conwaymaritime.com or contact:

Conway
151 Freston Road
London W10 6TH
Tel: +44 (0)20 7314 1400
Fax: +44 (0)20 7314 1594

An imprint of Anova Books Company Ltd

AIR COMBAT SUPPORT

A Tornado demonstrates how the probe-and-drogue system operates in flight

Number 2 Group is required to 'Project, Protect and Support' Force Elements on operations and exercises worldwide, which drives its unique collection of capabilities:

Project – by providing air transport and air-to-air refuelling capabilities to support the expeditionary posture of our agile Air Force.
Protect – by delivering Force Protection to deployed air assets through the activities of Air Combat Support Units such as RAF Regiment squadrons and the Tactical Provost Wing.
Support – by sustaining deployed air assets through the activities of Air Combat Service Support Units such as Tactical Communications Wing and the Mobile Catering Support Unit.

This complex and demanding remit is accomplished through a wide variety of units operating eight types of aircraft and a vast array of offensive and defensive equipment.

Number 2 Group's aircraft are tasked to support Defence in its broadest sense. The communications fleet, based at RAF Northolt, operates the BAe 125 and BAe 146 passenger aircraft and the Twin Squirrel helicopter, and provides Royal and VIP transport in direct support of operations worldwide. The air transport and air-to-air refuelling fleets are based at RAF Lyneham and RAF Brize Norton and operate the C-130 Hercules, VC10, TriStar and C-17 Globemaster. These aircraft provide a broad range of capabilities including strategic and tactical transport of passengers and freight, air-to-air refuelling, aerial delivery by parachute, and aeromedical evacuation. In addition to operations mounted from their UK bases, 2 Group maintain standing overseas detachments of its aircraft in locations ranging from the South Atlantic to the Middle East and Afghanistan.

The Air Combat Support Units provide our forces with ground defence and security, Short Range Air Defence, NBC warning and detection and, most importantly, the command and control facilities necessary to co-ordinate these activities. When they are not deployed on operations, the Regular and Auxiliary Squadrons of the RAF Regiment and the Operational Support Squadrons of the Royal Auxiliary Air Force, which are distributed across a variety of RAF stations throughout the UK, are grouped under the RAF Regiment Force Protection Wing Headquarters based at RAF Honington. The Joint RAF/Army NBC Regiment is also based at RAF Honington, while the Tactical Provost Wing is based at RAF Henlow.

The Air Combat Service Support Units provide a broad spectrum of capabilities to air deployments, including: deployable airfield radar facilities, catering, mechanical transport, logistics, armament support, bomb disposal, air movements staff, fire fighting, medical services and communications. The specialised units that deliver these capabilities are dispersed across a number of locations including RAF Wittering, RAF Stafford and RAF St Athan.

The future for 2 Group is exciting and includes the introduction of the A400M transport aircraft and the Future Strategic Tanker Aircraft (FSTA). The A400M will replace the Hercules C-130K and bridge the capability gap between the strategic lift capacity of the C-17 and the tactical capacity of the C-130J. The FSTA is a Private Finance Initiative contract and is currently being negotiated to replace the RAF's existing VC10 and TriStar air-to-air refuelling aircraft. The RAF is seeking to purchase a complete air-to-air refuelling service but it is envisaged that this fleet will also be utilised extensively to fly air transport missions, including those of aeromedical evacuation. ∎

Powerplant:

Three RR RB211 turbofans	
Thrust:	50,000lbs each
Wing span:	50.09m
Length:	50.05m
Height:	16.87m
Max T/O weight:	245 tonnes
Internal fuel:	96.9 tonnes
Max speed:	520kts
Max altitude:	43,000ft

The RAF has a mixed fleet of nine Lockheed L-1011 TriStar aircraft, which are operated by No 216 Squadron, based at RAF Brize Norton, Oxfordshire, in the air transport (AT) and air-to-air refuelling (AAR) roles. The aircraft, which previously saw airline service when they were owned by British Airways and Pan Am, were purchased by the RAF in the early 1980s. The six ex-British Airways aircraft were modified by Marshall of Cambridge (Engineering) into AAR tanker aircraft, with a twin, centreline hose-and-drogue configuration. Four aircraft were designated KC1, while two were designated K1. The installation includ-ed the addition of under-floor fuel tanks which increased the available fuel load by 43,900kgs. This allows a total fuel load of 139,700kgs to be carried, which can be used by the aircraft itself, or given away to receivers. AAR operations can be monitored by a CCTV system, which was added under the rear of the fuselage.

Although the aircraft has two hose-drum refuelling units, only one can be used at a time, thus restricting AAR to single-point refuelling. On a typical AAR flight from the UK to Cyprus, or Gander (Canada), the KC1 can refuel up to four fast-jet aircraft and simul-taneously carry up to 31 tonnes of passengers and/or freight. The addi-tion of a large, fuselage freight-door and a roller-conveyor system allow outsized palletised cargo to be car-ried. Although the K1 model does not have the freight door, it retains a pas-senger-seat fit of 187 in the rear cabin, with baggage carried in the forward cabin.

The three ex-Pan Am aircraft are largely unchanged from their airline days and operate in the passenger role, carrying up to 266 passengers. These aircraft are designated C2 and C2A and are used extensively for transporting troops to world-wide destinations in support of exercises and operations. All versions of the TriStar aircraft can operate in the aeromedical evacuation role, includ-ing the option of installing a full stretcher fit if required for the repatri-ation of casualties.

All RAF TriStars have a comprehen-sive avionics suite, which is undergo-ing modernisation. As part of this pro-gramme the aircraft are being fitted with equipment which will enable them to operate as a JTIDS (Joint Tactical Information Distribution System) station and a radio relay sta-tion in areas of intensive military oper-ations. ■

TriStar port profile

TriStar KC1 with its centreline
hose-and-drogue extended

ZD951

AIR FORCE

Powerplant:

Four RR Conway turbofans

Thrust:	20,000lbs each
Wingspan:	44.55m
Length:	48.36m
Max T/O weight:	152tonnes
Range:	5000nmls
Speed:	530kts
Ceiling:	43,000ft

The VC10 C1K is a dual-role AT and AAR aircraft. In the AT role, the aircraft is used for troop carrying, with accommodation for 124 passengers and nine crew. Use of a large, cabin-freight door on the forward left side of the aircraft allows easy conversion of the aircraft into a dual-role passenger/freight or full-freight configuration. In its full-freight role, the cabin can hold up to 20,400kgs of palletised freight, ground equipment or vehicles, on its permanently strengthened floor. The aircraft can also be used for aero-medical evacuation, for which up to 68 stretchers may be fitted.

The C1Ks were converted to the AAR role in 1993 with the fitting of a Mk32 refuelling pod under the outboard section of each wing. The aircraft can carry up to 69,800kgs of fuel using its original eight fuel tanks; the fuel can be used to feed the aircraft itself or be dispensed to receiver aircraft that are equipped with a probe-and-drogue refuelling system. Capable of refuelling two aircraft simultaneously from the two underwing pods, the VC10 C1K can itself be refuelled from a suitably equipped VC10K or TriStar AAR aircraft by the use of an air-to-air refuelling probe, which is permanently attached to the aircraft nose. The aircraft is equipped with a modern flight-management system and the avionics required for full worldwide operations. The crew comprises two pilots, a weapon systems officer, a flight engineer, an air loadmaster and up to three air stewards.

The bulk of the RAF's single-role AAR fleet comprises VC10s of two different variants, the K3 and K4. Each aircraft is a three-point tanker, with fuel being dispensed from the two wing-hoses or from the single fuselage-mounted Hose Drum Unit (HDU). The wing hoses can transfer fuel at up to 1000kgs per minute and are used to refuel tactical fast-jet aircraft. The HDU can transfer fuel up to 2000kgs per minute and is usually used to refuel 'heavy' strategic aircraft, although it can also be used by fast-jet aircraft.

Each tanker variant of VC10 carries a different fuel load. The K3 is equipped with fuselage fuel tanks, mounted in the passenger compartment, and can carry up to 78 tonnes of fuel. These internal tanks are not fitted to the K4, which has a maximum fuel load of 68 tonnes. For self defence, the aircraft's only countermeasures are its recent change to a low infrared paint scheme (grey), a radar-warning receiver and a Matador IRCM (Infrared Counter Measures) missile-protection system, which comprises two infrared jammers mounted under the engines at the rear of the aircraft. The aircraft also has a very limited passenger-carrying capacity

VC10 port profile

A line of VC10s on the tarmac in the Gulf

used almost exclusively to carry ground crew and other operational support personnel.

The VC10 is now reaching the end of its service life, but continual modifications maintain the aircraft as a significant asset, enabling the rapid deployment of troops and their weaponry, and fast-jet fighter aircraft, to any theatre of operations around the world. ■

Powerplant:	Four P&W
	F117- PW-100 turbofans
Thrust:	40,400lbs each
Wingspan:	52m
Length:	53m
Height:	16.79m
Max T/O weight:	266tonnes
Max range:	4700nmls
Speed:	550kts
Ceiling:	45,000ft

The C-17 Globemaster III is the latest addition to the RAF's inventory of transport aircraft. It is capable of rapid, strategic delivery of troops and all types of cargo to main operating bases anywhere in the world, or directly to more temporary forward operating bases owing to its short field capability. The design of the aircraft allows it to carry out high-angle, steep approaches at relatively slow speeds, thus allowing it to operate into small, austere airfields onto runways as short as 3,500 feet long and only 90 feet wide. The aircraft can operate into and out of problematic sites such as those surrounded by inhospitable terrain or made difficult by adverse weather conditions. The fully-integrated, electronic flight-deck and the advanced cargo-handling systems allow a basic crew of only two pilots and one air loadmaster to operate the aircraft. On the ground, the aircraft can be turned in a very small radius and its four Pratt & Whitney engines are fully reversible, giving it the ability to manoeuvre into and out of restricted parking or freight-offload areas at undeveloped strips. This enables the C-17 to deliver cargo to small airfields with limited parking space in a shorter time, so increasing throughput where time on the ground is kept to a minimum. The C-17 can transport 45,360kgs of freight over 4,500 nautical miles whilst flying at heights in excess of 30,000 feet.

Cargo is loaded on to the C-17 through a large rear door that can accommodate military vehicles and palletised cargo. It can carry almost all of the Army's air-transportable, out-sized combat equipment, from three Warrior armoured vehicles or 13 Land Rovers, to a Chinook helicopter or three Apache-sized helicopters. It carries all its own role-equipment and can fit centre-line seating, which increases the seating capacity from 54 side-wall seats to 102 seats. The aircraft can also be configured in the aeromedical evacuation role to carry a full stretcher fit. The C-17 needs little or no ground support equipment and if none is available it can perform a combat off-load where pallets are dropped from the aircraft ramp on to the taxiway or hardstanding.

The C-17 gives the RAF a long-range strategic heavy-lift transport aircraft that offers the ability to project and sustain an effective force close to a potential area of operations for combat, peacekeeping or humanitarian missions worldwide. The aircraft is a declared part of the UK's Joint Rapid Reaction Force and the RAF is currently the only European force which can offer 'outsize airlift' assets from within its own inventory. In 2004 the MoD announced the intention to buy the current fleet of four aircraft at the conclusion of the current lease arrangement in 2008 and to purchase one additional aircraft; bringing our C-17 fleet up to five. ■

C-17 Globemaster III port profile

A C-17 at night in the Gulf, showing off its wide-track undercarriage and powerful engines, which provide a brisk short-field performance

Powerplant:	Four EPI TP400-D6 turboprops
Thrust:	11,000shp each
Propeller:	8-blade variable pitch fully feathering
Wing span:	42.4m
Tailplane span:	19.65m
Length:	42.2m
Height:	14.7m
Max range:	4100nmls
Speed:	510kts
Ceiling:	40,000ft

The current mainstays of the RAF's tactical and strategic airlift are the C-130 Hercules aircraft and the C-17 Globemaster. The A400M is being designed to bridge the gap between strategic and tactical operations. The aircraft is being developed by a seven-nation partnership: Belgium; France; Luxembourg; Germany; Spain; Turkey and UK. These nations signed a contract for 180 of the resulting A400M in 2003 – of which 25 will go to the RAF with an aircraft in-service date expected early next decade. The seven partner nations have also agreed to work together to harmonise the selection of ground equipment and spares, many of which will be common to

A400Ms prepare for take-off in this Airbus artist's impression

other civil Airbus aircraft fleets.

The aircraft has the nominal ability to carry a 25 tonne payload over 3,000nmls to remote civilian and military airfields; furthermore, the range of the aircraft can be extended by the use of a removable air-refueling probe mounted above the cockpit. Troops (up to 116 paratroopers) and cargo can be dropped simultaneously either by parachute or gravity extraction, or by landing on short, unprepared or semi-prepared strips. A single loadmaster will control the cargo bay, which has a five tonne capacity crane

A400M port profile

ROYAL AIR FORCE
400
400
ZA400

Airbus A400M: artist's impression of operations from rough and unsupported strips

at the rear to handle military pallets. The aircraft will be capable of operating either at low-level (down to 150ft agl) or at high-level altitudes up to 40,000ft.

The two-pilot flight-deck crew will have the benefit of state-of-the-art equipment taken from other Airbus programmes, including sidestick controllers to operate the advanced fly-by-wire system and advanced structural design incorporating extensive use of composites. Additional systems will provide a night-vision compatible glass cockpit complete with two head-up displays supported by

at least five multi-function displays that will allow state-of-the-art avionics developments to be incorporated into the flight-deck design, so greatly reducing crew workload. The engines that will power the aircraft are four Europrop International (EPI) turboprops, each rated at over 10,000 horsepower and using huge composite propellers with a diameter of 5.3m. Unusually, the inboard and outboard propellers rotate in different directions, improving airflow and leading to a reduction in the size of the tailplane. The wings themselves are due to be manufactured in Bristol in

the UK and will be the largest to use composite technology.

A modern defensive-aids suite will be fitted, incorporating radar and missile warning receivers, electronic countermeasure equipment and chaff/flare dispensers. The cargo bay of the A400M can be configured for a number of roles: pure troop carrying, or a mixture of troops and support equipment; palletised cargo or military wheeled and tracked vehicles; two attack helicopters such as the Apache or Puma; or a mixture of light and heavy engineering equipment. ■

Powerplant: Four Allison T56-A-15 turboprops
Thrust: 4200shp each
Propeller: Hamilton hydromatic four-blade constant speed propeller
Wing span: 40.38m
Tailplane span: 16.04m
Length: 29.77m (CMk1)
34.89m (CMk3)
Range: 3000nmls
Speed: 310kts
Ceiling: 32,000ft

The C-130 Hercules tactical transport aircraft is the workhorse of the RAF's Air Transport (AT) fleet and is based at RAF Lyneham, in Wiltshire, where it is operated by Nos 24, 30, 47 and 70 Squadrons. Also based at RAF Lyneham is No 57(R) Squadron, which is the Hercules Operational Conversion Unit. The fleet totals 50 aircraft and is a mixture of C1/C3 aircraft and the new C-130J aircraft, designated C4/C5.

The C1 and C3 aircraft are used primarily to carry troops, passengers or freight and are capable of carrying up to 128 passengers, or 20 tonnes of palletised freight or vehicles, for up to 2000nmls. The freight bay can accommodate a range of wheeled or tracked vehicles, or up to seven pallets of general freight. In the aeromedical evacuation role either 64 or 82 stretchers can be carried, depending on the mark of aircraft and the stretcher configuration. The maximum unrefuelled ferry range is 3500nmls, which can be extended to over 4000nmls by air-to-air refuelling.

The other main role of the C-130 is Transport Support (TS), which is the airborne delivery of personnel or stores by airdrop. In this role the aircraft supports airborne operations conducted by 16 Air Assault Brigade by the aerial delivery of paratroops, stores and equipment. The aircraft is particularly valuable in its TS role as it can be operated from unprepared and semi-prepared surfaces by day or by night.

The majority of aircraft are fitted with defensive infrared countermeasure equipment, whilst some aircraft used for special tasks have an additional, enhanced defensive-aids suite comprising a Skyguardian radar-warning receiver, a chaff and flare countermeasure dispensing system and a missile approach warning system. The C3 is also equipped with station-keeping equipment, which enables the aircraft to maintain its airborne position in a large formation in thick cloud or bad weather where the other formation members cannot be seen. The aircraft are receiving an ongoing avionics, electrical and structural upgrade, which will enable them to remain the workhorse of the AT fleet into the next decade. ∎

Hercules C-130K C1/C3 port profile

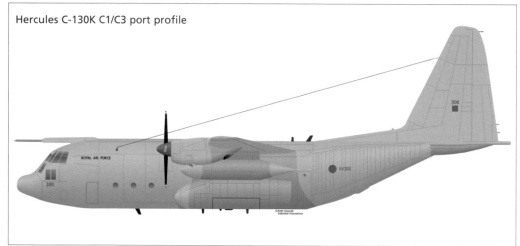

An RAF Hercules C-130K over the desert

Powerplant: Four Allison AE
2100D3 turboprops
Thrust: 4700shp each
Propeller: Dowty R39
six-blade variable pitch
propeller
Wing span: 40.38m
Tailplane span: 16.04m
Length: 34.34m (C4)
29.77m (C5)
Range: 3000nmls
Speed: 340kts
Ceiling: 32,000ft

The RAF has a total of 25 C-130J C4/C5 aircraft. The C4 is almost the same size as the current C3 aircraft, but with a slightly shorter fuselage, while the C5 is the same size as the C1. The C-130J has been modified and upgraded to include new Allison AE turboprop engines and Dowty Aerospace six-bladed composite propellers. The new engines and advanced propellers, coupled with a new digital engine-control system, give the C-130J increased take-off thrust and better fuel efficiency; thus the external fuel tanks have been omitted. The aircraft also has a revised flight deck with modern glass-cockpit and head-up displays, allowing two-pilot, flight deck operation. The cockpit of the aircraft is fully night-vision compatible with the use of night-vision goggles. A separate air loadmaster station has been established in the cargo hold. The aircraft has been cleared for wider use in the tactical TS role and is used for operational missions involving parachute ops and air despatch.

The defensive-aids suite includes a missile warning system linked to the directional, infrared countermeasure system, a radar warning receiver and a chaff and flare dispensing system. The defensive system helps protect the aircraft against surface-to-air and air-to-air infrared seeking weapons that may be encountered during operations. ∎

The modern cockpit of the Hercules C-130J

A Hercules C-130J over the British countryside; note the lack of external wing-mounted fuel packs

Powerplant:	4 Avco Lycoming ALF502R-5 turbofans
Thrust:	6790lbs each
Wing span:	26.8m
Length:	26.18m
Height:	8.61m
Max T/O weight:	37tonnes
Max fuel:	10,300kg
Speed:	300kts
Ceiling:	30,000ft

The BAE 146 CC2 is operated by No 32 (The Royal) Squadron, at RAF Northolt. The Squadron operates two BAE 146s in the Royal or VVIP transport and communication roles. The standard operating crew for each aircraft consists of two pilots, two cabin crew and a ground engineer.

The BAE 146 CC2 is an all-metal, high-wing monoplane, with a wide-bodied fuselage and a slightly swept, anhedral wing. The fin is also slightly swept with a high T-tail. Ailerons and elevators are controlled through conventional wire-linked servo tabs, whereas the rudder is hydraulically operated. The secondary flight-controls are hydraulically powered and include a large airbrake on the rear fuselage, and single slotted flaps and lift spoilers on the upper wing. The aircraft is powered by four Avco Lycoming ALF502R-5 turbofans that have a 6:1 bypass ratio. Numbers one and four engines supply the aircraft's electrical power, while numbers two and three engines drive the aircraft's hydraulic pumps. The aircraft has a trailing-axle main gear with a large damper unit, which allows the aircraft to operate from unprepared surfaces, including gravel and desert runways. The aircraft's excellent performance provides good short-field capability and allows it to operate from airfields located at up to 14,000ft above sea level. The aircraft is based on the civilian BAE 146 100 Series, but has additional fuel tanks and a Royal Suite cabin-fit; and the modern, electronic defensive-aids suite gives almost 360° protection against infrared missiles.

The BAE 146 CC2 is fitted with three passenger compartments.

A BAE 146 banks away to port

Compartment A is situated at the front of the aircraft and accommodates the crew. Compartment B, in the centre of the fuselage, accommodates additional crew and extra passengers. Compartment C is situated at the rear of the aircraft and accommodates Royal or VVIP passengers. The layout of the compartments can be varied to meet task requirements, but the maximum seating capacity is 30 passengers.

The BAE 146 is a quiet but rugged aircraft, with a high level of built-in redundancy. It can carry many of its own spares, allowing it to operate for long periods away from base, with little or no external support. The aircraft's excellent short-field performance, and its ability to operate from high or unprepared airfields in missile threat areas, mean that the aircraft is extremely versatile. ■

BAE 146, in Royal Squadron colours, port profile

The HS125 CC3 is operated by No 32 (The Royal) Squadron, at RAF Northolt. The Squadron operates six Series 700B aircraft in the Royal or VIP transport and communication roles. The standard operating crew for each aircraft consists of two pilots and one cabin attendant.

The HS125 CC3 is an all-metal, low-wing monoplane with a semi-monocoque fuselage and a moderately swept, cantilever wing and stabilisers. It is certified as a transport category aircraft and can operate in all weather conditions, including adverse icing conditions. The aircraft is powered by two Garrett TFE731-3-1H turbofans that are attached by pylons to the rear section of the aircraft. The lightweight TFE series of engines are quiet and economical and their modular design allows easy maintenance and reduces the engine's unserviceability rate. In addition to providing power, the engines also drive an accessory gearbox, which, in turn, drives the aircraft's fuel, oil and hydraulic pumps and a generator for electrical power. As each engine has a separate gearbox, all aircraft systems can operate normally on a single engine. The HS125 CC3 is also fitted with an electronic

defensive-aids suite that gives the aircraft almost 360° protection against infrared missiles.

The HS125 fuselage contains three main sections. The forward section of the fuselage contains a weather radar, the cockpit and the galley area; the centre section contains the passenger compartment, which can accommodate up to six passengers and their luggage; the rear section contains a large equipment bay and two additional fuel tanks for extended-range operations.

The HS125 CC3 regularly provides a passenger service to the Royal Family, Government ministers and senior military officers. Its robust engineering, flexibility of operation

HS125 on operations in the Balkans

and rapid turn-around times have made it a very successful aircraft, operated throughout the world in the VIP role and, in its communications role, the HS125 CC3 has provided support for most RAF peacekeeping and humanitarian operations worldwide. ■

Powerplant:	Two Garrett TFE731-3-1H turbofans
Thrust:	7400lbs total
Wing span:	14.33m
Length:	15.46m
Height:	5.49m
Max T/O weight:	11,590kg
Speed:	320kts
Ceiling:	41,000ft

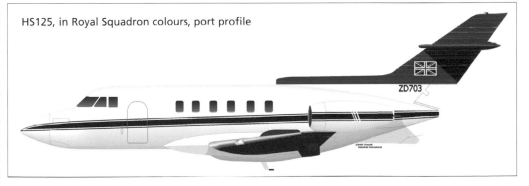

HS125, in Royal Squadron colours, port profile

ZD703

Royal Squadron Twin Squirrel VIP transport & communication

Powerplant:	Two Allison
	250 C20 turboshafts
Thrust:	420shp each
Length:	12.94m
Height:	3.02m
Rotor span:	10.69m
Max T/O weight:	2400kg
Speed:	150kts
Ceiling:	16,000ft

Three AS 355 F1 Aerospatiale Twin Squirrel helicopters are operated by No 32 (The Royal) Squadron, at RAF Northolt, as replacements for the Gazelle in the VIP transport and communication roles. The Twin Squirrel is operated by a single pilot.

The aircraft is a twin-engined, six-seat helicopter with a skid undercarriage, and is derived from the single-engined AS 350B Single Squirrel design. The rotor system is made up of three main rotor blades of glass-resin laminate construction, a starflex semi-rigid main rotor-head, a two-bladed glass-resin laminate tail rotor, and main-rotor and tail-rotor gearboxes of conventional geared design. The Twin Squirrel has two independent hydraulic circuits: one for the upper body of the main servo, and the other for the lower body of the main servo and the tail servo unit. The airframe comprises an aluminium

Twin Squirrel is used in the VIP transport role; seen here banking over the Thames at Tower Bridge

centre fuselage and cabin floor, a monocoque tailboom, a fibreglass-laminated cabin ceiling and main cowlings, and polycarbonate windows. Built by Eurocopter France, and first certified by the UK Civil Aviation Authority in March 1984, the helicopter can be used by day and by night, in all weather conditions. It has full instrumentation and navigation systems, including a three-axis autopilot, an auto-coupled Instrument Landing System and a satellite-based Global Positioning System.

The Twin Squirrel is powered by two Allison 250 C20 turboshaft engines, installed in two independent fireproof bays. The well-proven, reliable engines drive fuel, oil and hydraulic pumps, and a generator for

all electrical power. The twin-engine design gives the pilot more flexibility when planning routes over built-up areas, as the aircraft can operate at limited weight on a single engine; therefore, even if power from one engine is lost, the pilot can maintain level flight to clear the built-up area. The twin-engine design also increases safety margins when flying into and out of confined landing sites.

The Twin Squirrels of No 32 (The Royal) Squadron are leased to the RAF under a civilian-owned, military-regulated arrangement. This arrangement allows the RAF to provide Government ministers and senior military officers with a flexible, door-to-door service throughout the UK and to Europe. ■

Twin Squirrel, in Royal Squadron colours, port profile

RAF Regiment

Raised in 1942, the Royal Air Force Regiment is the RAF's specialist airfield defence corps. Its history is directly linked to the Number 1 Armoured Car Company which was formed in 1921. The Regiment serves as the role model for many other nations' airfield defence organisations. With squadrons and wing headquarters held permanently on high operational readiness, the Regiment is a key component of the UK's Joint Rapid Reaction Force. Air transportable, and with one of the squadrons parachute-capable, the Regiment is a highly mobile and versatile force that can quickly be projected worldwide to defend expeditionary air forces or carry out other tasks. Squadrons are capable of independent operations or can be grouped together in wings to provide increased mass or a wider range of capabilities. The Regiment has Rapier Field Standard C (Rapier FSC) anti-aircraft missile squadrons to defend against air attack, field squadrons to conduct offensive action against ground attackers, and Force Protection Wing Headquarters to provide command and control of the many force protection elements found on a deployed operating base. On operations these units can be reinforced from Royal Auxiliary Air Force (RAuxAF) Regiment Squadrons or Operational Support Squadrons of the RAuxAF. The Regiment also makes up a significant proportion of the Joint CBRN Regiment, the Defence CBRN Centre, provides Tactical Air Control Parties for Army units,

An RAF Regiment gunner provides cover while troops board a Chinook helicopter

defends key assets in Cyprus, and mans the newly formed Ground Extraction Force, which is tasked to recover downed aircrew that have landed within reach of the enemy. The experience gained on these front line units is carried across to the Force Protection Centre at RAF Honington and the Regiment training teams present on every RAF station and major training establishment, who provide the force protection and pre-deployment training that ensures personnel of the wider RAF are able to play their part in the defence of deployed airfields. Irrespective of their employment, all Regiment personnel are trained to be primarily ground close-combat specialists and maintain a high level of skill in this area. ■

An RAF Regiment Rapier Ground-Based Air Defence system deployed in the Gulf

Force Protection and Ground Combat Units

Force Protection Wing Headquarters

Tactically mobile and able to operate with the minimum of infrastructure, a Force Protection Wing HQ will be one of the first units on the ground. Its role is to provide the command and control of the numerous units that contribute to the Force Protection of the deployed air operation. A key task is to ensure that these units are fully integrated in order that the maximum possible effect is achieved. At the reconnaissance stage before any deployment, its staff will evaluate the threats and hazards facing the deploying force and produce the Force Protection plan before any aircraft arrive. During expeditionary operations this planning will involve liaison with other coalition members and host nation forces; therefore, it requires individuals with an understanding of the strategic context in which they work, a wide-ranging operational experience and well developed interpersonal skills. The skills and experience of HQ staff are also optimised to support the specific and often unique requirements of deployed air operations. This helps HQs to train and prepare other elements of the RAF to operate from deployed bases where there is a threat of attack and to provide advice to allied air forces. Routinely grouped under each of the six Force Protection Wing HQs is a RAF Regiment field squadron, a RAuxAF Regiment field squadron and/or a RAuxAF Operational Support Squadron. However, the HQ is an inherently flexible organisation that can and does take command of many other units, such as RAF Police, Joint CBRN Regt, Fire, Medical, EOD and Royal Engineer units, that may be required for the force protection task. ∎

Regiment briefing prior to a mission in Basrah

51 Squadron ready to deploy in Iraq

RAF Regiment Field Squadrons

Field Squadrons Structure
Men: 171

Flights
HQ Flight: 1
Manoeuvre Support Flight: 1
Rifle Flights: 3
Combat Service Support Flight: 1

Vehicles
Land Rover Wolf: 38
   (including a number of Weapon
         Mount Installation Kits)
4-tonne trucks: 17
8-tonne trucks: 2
Motorcycles: 5

Weapons
5.56mm Individual Weapon:
                              1 per man
40mm Under-barrel Grenade
Launcher (for above):   18
5.56mm Light Support Weapon: 24
5.56mm Minimi Light
Machine Gun: 18
7.62mm General Purpose
Machine Gun: 24
Sustained Fire Kits (for above):   9
81mm Mortar: 4
51mm Mortar: 4
L96 7.62mm Sniper Rifle: 4
Javelin Anti-Tank Missile

II Squadron parachute drop

Surveillance equipment
MSTAR (ground surveillance radar)
Spyglass (thermal imaging sight)
Common Weapon Sight (image intensifier)
Maxi-Kite (image intensifier)
SOPHIE (hand-held thermal imaging sight)
Hand-Held Laser Rangefinder
CLASSIC (seismic and Infra-Red intrusion detector)
Helmet-Mounted Night Vision System
Laser Aimer Torch (for Individual Weapons)

RAF Regiment field squadrons are highly mobile units that are able to deploy globally at very short notice and operate in all weathers by day and night. They are a key part of the RAF's force protection construct and, as an intrinsic element of the Service they integrate seamlessly with other force protection elements to deliver a significantly enhanced effect. There are six regular RAF Regiment field squadrons: Numbers 1, II, 3, 34, 51 and 63 squadrons. Number II Squadron is also parachute-capable. The increasing capability and cost of modern military combat aircraft means that fewer aircraft need to be deployed on operations and the effect that they have is out of proportion to their numbers. This also means that these aircraft and their supporting elements will be high priority targets for adversaries. The exceptional challenges of defending an airfield, densely packed with high value assets, requires a specialist capability to detect and defeat threats before they can impact on the conduct of air operations. These challenges could include infiltration or long-range attacks or attempts to shoot down aircraft with man-portable air defence systems during their approach or departure from the airfield. Although externally similar to Infantry counterparts, the training, equipment and tactics of a field squadron are unique and are optimised to deal decisively with likely threats to air operations. A field squadron is very heavily armed with indirect fire systems, such as mortars, and direct fire weapons including machine guns, sniper rifles and anti-tank missiles. Each squadron has a comprehensive suite of surveillance equipment which allows it to detect and identify friendly, neutral and hostile activity within its area of operations and to rapidly direct action against adversaries. The training of RAF Regiment personnel on field squadrons allows them to undertake predominantly covert observation and patrolling activity, although in certain circumstances overt activity is also used. This gives the squadrons the ability to identify threats early and then undertake offensive action using a combination of fire and manoeuvre to fix and strike adversaries. The tactics and procedures routinely employed by field squadrons are specifically designed to accommodate the singular requirements of air operations, although they are also capable of employing standard Infantry doc-

A personal weapon – the L85 5.56mm rifle

The three RAuxAF Regiment field squadrons (2503, 2620 and 2622 squadrons) are manned by volunteers from civilian employment, who accept a liability to be called out for service in certain circumstances. Each squadron has 129 men and is similarly organised to a Regular field squadron, less the manoeuvre support flight. Members train for a minimum of 27 days per year alongside their Regular counterparts and deploy either or in small teams to reinforce Regular units or potentially as formed units in their own right. The last major deployment of Auxiliary field squadron was to Kuwait and Iraq on Operation Telic during the Iraq war and small numbers continue to support ongoing operations in the Middle East. ■

Rapid and heavy fire is provided by the 7.62mm calibre GPMG

trine and tactics if required for other roles. The size and structure of a field squadron and its ability to operate independently makes it ideally suited for discrete tasks, such as Non-Combatant Evacuation Operations, where speed of deployment and ability to operate across the spectrum of conflict are paramount. Number 63 Squadron RAF Regiment is also known as the Queen's Colour Squadron. Based at RAF Uxbridge it carries out major ceremonial duties on behalf of the RAF at home and abroad, including periodically guarding the London palaces, the Tower of London and Windsor Castle. Both 3 and 63 Squadrons are in the process of increasing in size to adopt the same strength and structure as the other field squadrons. In recent years, field squadrons have participated in operations in Afghanistan, Bosnia, Croatia, Cyprus, Iraq, Kenya, Kosovo, Kuwait, Macedonia, Northern Ireland, and Sierra Leone. They also routinely train in a wide variety of terrain and climatic conditions, including urban areas, jungle, desert and extreme cold weather. ■

GBAD Squadrons

Structure
Men: 106

Flights:
HQ Flight   1
Engineering Flight   1
Rapier Flight   2

Vehicles:
Land Rovers   11
4-tonne/8-tonne trucks   32

Weapons:
Rapier launchers   6
7.62mm GPMGs   7
5.56mm L85A2   1 per man

Surveillance Assets:
Rapier Thermo-Electro
Optical tracker
Dagger surveillance radar
(range 16km)
Tracking radar (range 16km)
Common Weapon Sight
(Image Intensifier)

There are three Rapier GBAD squadrons (15, 16 and 26 squadrons), all identically manned and equipped. After 2008, the GBAD role will be carried out by the Royal Artillery as the number of units required to perform this role against a reduced threat is judged to be smaller. All RAF Regiment personnel will be moved to other employment within the Regiment and the overall strength will not decrease. The squadrons are currently declared operationally to NATO's Supreme Allied Commander Europe and are held at very high readiness to deploy worldwide in order to protect early entry forces of all three Services. To maintain these high standards, the squadrons remain permanently in-role and are subject to annual evaluations by the GBAD Force Headquarters and NATO evaluators. The Royal Artillery will adopt this best practice in the future when they assume responsibility for all GBAD. Squadrons routinely train in Arctic and desert conditions to maintain their flexibility. Rapier is a 24-hour, all-weather weapon system with a radar detection range of 9nmls and a missile range of 5nmls. The equipment is extremely mobile and can be air transported inside a C-130 Hercules or car-

Rapier missiles fly at over 1500 metres per second to their targets

ried underneath Sea King and Chinook helicopters. The Rapier FSC can detect aircraft or cruise missile targets, either by using its own tracking radar or by an operator-controlled thermal electro-optics system. The missile is highly resistant to electronic countermeasures, flies at speeds in excess of 1500 metres per second and, when equipped with a proximity fuse, it has a very high success rate against most targets. The launcher carries up to eight missiles that are radar guided during flight and have

both proximity and kinetic fuses. The RAF GBAD Force deployed a squadron to the Falkland Islands during the conflict in 1982 and has maintained elements continuously in the Falklands since then. RAF Rapier squadrons also deployed to Saudi Arabia and Bahrain during the first Gulf War in 1991 and in the most recent Gulf conflict deployed to Kuwait and Iraq, where a number of roles were carried out including air defence to Army units in the manoeuvre battle. ■

RAF Regiment Specialist Units

Joint Chemical Biological Radiological and Nuclear (CBRN) Regiment

Number 27 Squadron RAF Regiment makes up one quarter of the manpower of the Joint CBRN Regiment, which provides the UK's armed services with its CBRN reconnaissance, identification and decontamination capability. Elements of the squadron are parachute trained in order that this can be conducted alongside other airborne forces. The Squadron is currently equipped with the Prototype Biological Detection System (PBDS) and is helping to introduce its replacement, the Integrated Biological Detection System (IBDS). PBDS provides the means to detect a biological attack and brings the science of the laboratory into the field. IBDS will be a marked improvement in capability and is currently being procured by the MoD. Whilst the Joint CBRN Regiment is a centrally controlled asset, elements of it might be detached to support a deployed operating base and their employment will be co-ordinated by the Force Protection Wing Headquarters. In times of crisis, the Regiment can be augmented with personnel of 2623 Squadron RAuxAF Regiment. The Squadron was extensively deployed throughout the Gulf region in the recent Iraq war, and continues to provide support to operations worldwide, playing a crucial part of UK forces allocated to NATO.

Operational Support Squadrons

Although not part of the RAF Regiment, the Operational Support Squadrons provide individuals and teams with specialist force protection skills to the Force Protection Wing Headquarters. Examples of such skills include combined incident teams, guard commanders, NBC plotters, and NBC shelter marshals. Additionally, they provide reinforcements to field squadrons and contribute to Tactical Psychological Operations Teams. The operations support squadrons are part of the RAuxAF; therefore, they are manned with volunteers from civilian life.

Force Protection Centre/Common Core Skills Training

The RAF Force Protection Centre's operational role requires it to deploy teams equipped to sample any biological, chemical or radioactive agent found by a CBRN reconnaissance team, and then to transport it to specialist facilities for detailed analysis. It also provides advice to the

An 81mm mortar in action at night

NBC protection exercise

The 81mm mortar has a range of 5000 metres

Home Office on CBRN-related issues and gives pre-deployment force protection briefs to operational commanders. The Centre provides enhanced Individual Reinforcement training for RAF personnel and others deploying to high threat environments. On RAF stations, teams of RAF Regiment officers and NCOs deliver annual force protection and pre-deployment training packages to all RAF personnel. These packages are produced by the Force Protection Centre, which also conducts annual assessments of each training team to ensure that training standards are maintained. Within the Centre is the Force Protection Tactics and Trials Development Unit.

RAF Combat Recovery

The RAF Regiment provides the Ground Extraction Force for the RAF Combat Recovery mission and is tasked to recover isolated personnel and high-value assets, by day or night, in all threat levels over extended periods. Small teams from the Ground Extraction Force are inserted primarily by Merlin HC3 helicopters to locate, authenticate and recover the isolated person or asset. Teams are self-sufficient and can operate behind enemy

Field Squadron sniper with L96 rifle operating in the desert

lines, utilising RAF Regiment tactics and certain items of specialist equipment. Operational environments will include desert, arctic, mountain, jungle and urban, in high threat levels. The Ground Extraction Force is a part of E Flight, 28 (AC) Squadron and is based at RAF Benson.

Tactical Air Control Parties

The RAF Regiment provides a number of Tactical Air Control Parties (TACPs) for the Army's Mechanised and 16 Air Assault Brigades. The 16 Brigade teams are parachute trained for the airborne insertion role. Each team comprises a junior officer, a senior NCO and two gunners, and is equipped with state-of-the-art laser target designators, laser range finders, global positioning satellite receivers, infrared aiming devices and ground-to-ground and ground-to-air radios. Although an important part of the TACPs' role is the Forward Air Control of close support aircraft delivering weapons onto an enemy position, their task encompasses liaison between land and air force elements, and the management of the air battlespace to co-ordinate the activities of fast jets, attack helicopters, casualty evacuation missions and unmanned aerial vehicles.

Regiment Training Wing

The Regiment Training Wing provides specialist initial and postgraduate training for RAF Regiment gunners and officers. The Trainee Gunner Course lasts 22 weeks and covers initial recruit and basic infantry training, with an emphasis on practical skills. The 37-week Junior Regiment Officer Course is completed by newly-commissioned officers and teaches field craft, tactics, weapon skills and rangework, developing and testing leadership in a number of demanding exercises. In addition, the Wing delivers further training for field squadron executives, those gunners and junior NCOs selected for promotion, it also teaches those specialist skills required on a field squadron, such as sniper courses, and delivers all communications and signals training for the Regiment. All of the Wing's courses ensure that the students are capable of integrating seamlessly with other force protection elements and are well-prepared to contribute to the delivery of air operations. A small but important part of the Wing is the RAF Regiment Presentation Team, which tours the country publicising the role and capabilities of the Regiment.

Joint Rapier Training Unit

The Joint Rapier Training Unit delivers all Rapier Field Standard C training for the RAF and the Army, and is manned by instructors from the RAF Regiment and the Royal Artillery. Courses range from the Basic Operator's Course to the year-long Qualified Weapons Instructor's Course for selected officers and senior NCOs. All training is comprehensive and carefully validated to ensure that Rapier crews are able to operate their complex weapon systems to the full extent of its capability, and without endangering the friendly aircraft they are tasked to protect. The Training unit will disband in 2007 as the GBAD training role migrates to the Royal Artillery. All Regiment personnel will be transferred to other Regiment employment. ■

The 51mm mortar has a range of 800 metres

GBAD Rapier training on exercise

RAF RESERVES

4624 Sqn RAuxAF personnel with 624 Sqn RAF
Veterans at a D-Day ceremony in Southern France

RAF Reserves

The Royal Auxiliary Air Force (RAuxAF) celebrated its 80th birthday in 2004. It was one of Lord Trenchard's visions as far back as 1917 that there should be regionally raised forces made up of part-time volunteers that would form an Air Force Reserve. Civilians would give up some of their spare time, mainly at weekends, to train in a whole range of jobs. Throughout WWII, and in every conflict situation since then, auxiliaries have served in support of the RAF with great distinction. Reservists were put to the test more recently in 2003 when the RAuxAF was mobilised to support the RAF operations, during Operation Telic, in Iraq. This was the RAuxAF's first major mobilisation since WWII and 75% of all trained RAuxAF personnel were called out for periods of between four to six months. Many served overseas and in other key support positions at home.

Lord Trenchard's vision of part-time volunteers supporting the regular RAF has been amply vindicated. No longer an occasionally useful addition to the RAF's front line; the RAuxAF has earned its place as an essential part of it. Today, auxiliaries display the same enthusiasm, professionalism and commitment, as did their illustrious forebears. The original Auxiliary Air Force squadrons were formed under the auspices of County or Territorial Associations and they retain these important regional links to this day. ■

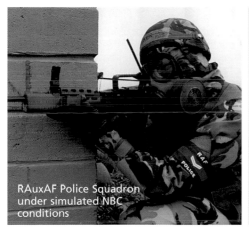

RAuxAF Police Squadron under simulated NBC conditions

RAuxAF 'digging in' at Ali Al Salem air base during the Iraq war

Following the major disbandment of Auxiliary Air Force Squadrons in the late 1950s, the renaissance of the RAuxAF began in 1979 with the formation of three Regiment Field Squadrons. Numerous squadrons were formed over the next 20 years and the total strength now comprises 21 squadrons covering all aspects of RAF support. A snapshot of the diverse roles of RAuxAF squadrons includes Operations Support, Helicopter Support, Surgical and Aeromedical Support, Movements Support plus a complete cross section of RAF Regiment and NBC Support. The RAuxAF also provides Communications and Intelligence Support and provides aircrew for 1359 Flight, the Hercules Reserve Aircrew Flight based at RAF Lyneham. During 2003, the RAuxAF was involved in the first large-scale mobilisation for over 50 years. More than 900 people, over 70% of its trained strength, were called into full-time service and were deployed to support RAF operations in Cyprus, Kuwait, Iraq and the Falkland Islands, as well as those in the UK. Details of the RAuxAF squadrons are as follows:

501 (COUNTY OF GLOUCESTER) SQUADRON

501 Squadron is an Operations Support Squadron based at RAF Brize Norton tasked with a primary role of Force Protection. The Squadron was mobilised in support of Operation Telic, and a total of 57 Squadron personnel deployed overseas to be employed on Force Protection duties; serving at coalition airbases located in eight different countries. Following the war-fighting phase, a contingent of 501 Squadron was deployed to help maintain security at Basrah International Airport.

504 (COUNTY OF NOTTINGHAM) SQUADRON

504 Squadron is an Operations Support Squadron (OSS) based at RAF Cottesmore. It has an establishment of 103 and recruits within a fifty-mile radius of Cottesmore. It is tasked with a primary role of Force Protection, which includes the provision of personnel trained as Guards, NBC Cell Controllers and Plotters, Shelter Marshals, and Combined Incident Team personnel. All of its trained personnel were deployed to bases within the Middle East during Operation Telic.

600 (CITY OF LONDON) SQUADRON

600 Squadron's role is to provide trained personnel to work in both RAF and Joint Headquarters worldwide. The Squadron, which is based at RAF Northolt, near Ruislip, has four flights: administration, communications, intelligence and operations. In 2003, up to one third of the Squadron was deployed in support of Operation Telic, mainly at locations in the UK, but with a number of personnel deployed to Iraq.

603 (CITY OF EDINBURGH) SQUADRON

603 Squadron was one of the first

three Auxiliary Squadrons to be raised in 1925, thus it has had links with the City of Edinburgh for 80 years. The primary role for the Squadron is Force Protection, but it also provides Mission Support for all RAF and NATO formations or units in today's concept of expeditionary warfare.

606 (CHILTERN) SQUADRON

606 Squadron is a Helicopter Support Squadron based at RAF Benson. The Squadron's role is to provide a pool of trained personnel to augment and reinforce the RAF Support Helicopter Force, which is a part of the tri-service Joint Helicopter Command. The Squadron provides Reservists trained in the operations, supply, transport, catering, general ground engineering and Regiment trades. The current establishment is for 180, including both permanent and part-time

staff. The Squadron has supported Operations in Albania, Kosovo, Bosnia, Kuwait and more recently, in Iraq.

609 (WEST RIDING) SQUADRON

The current role of the RAF Leeming based Squadron is to provide trained personnel to augment the RAF during operations, both in the UK and overseas, during times of crisis and war. The primary function of the Squadron is to provide personnel in the Force Protection role, integrating fully with their Regular counterparts. In February 2003, the Squadron was mobilised and deployed over 50 personnel to the Middle East, supporting operations in various locations.

612 (COUNTY OF ABERDEEN) SQUADRON

612 Squadron currently operates from RAF Leuchars, in Fife. The Squadron has an establishment of 79, allowing it to form two air-transportable surgical teams. The role of the Squadron is to provide field surgical support in times of conflict or war, and to provide peacetime surgical support to civilian populations in the event of major disaster. The unit has a 25-bed capacity, including two intensive treatment beds, and is capable of holding 25 patients for up to 48 hours.

2503 (COUNTY OF LINCOLN) SQUADRON
RAuxAF Regiment

2503 Squadron, the senior of the RAuxAF Regiment Squadrons, is based at RAF Waddington and provides a sustainment capability to the Regular RAF Regiment field squadrons. During Operation Telic, personnel from 2503 Squadron were deployed with II, 34 and 51 Squadrons RAF Regiment. Other Squadron personnel supported Force Protection operations at Ali Al Salem, in Kuwait, and at Basrah Airport, in Iraq.

2620 (COUNTY OF NORFOLK) SQUADRON
RAuxAF Regiment

2620 Squadron is an auxiliary RAF Regiment field squadron based in the UK. The Squadron was deployed to Ali Al Salem airbase in Kuwait in February 2003, where it provided part of the airbase's Force Protection component for the war-fighting phase of operation TELIC. The Squadron's role is to provide specialist auxiliary RAF Regiment manpower to augment the regular RAF Regiment field squadrons on RAF deployed Force Protection operations.

2622 (HIGHLAND) SQUADRON
RAuxAF Regiment

2622 Squadron, based at RAF Lossiemouth, is established for 121 auxiliary personnel, plus a small contingent of Regular RAF personnel. The Squadron's role is to provide a sustainment capability to the regular RAF Regiment field force squadrons. The Squadron supported Operation TELIC when Squadron personnel were attached to the Regular RAF Regiment squadrons. On commencement of war fighting operations, 51 Squadron RAF Regiment was one of the first British units to cross the Iraqi border with 2622 (Highland) members fully incorporated into the Regular Squadron's operational order of battle.

2623 (EAST ANGLIAN) SQUADRON
RAuxAF Regiment

2623 Squadron is part of the RAF's Ground Based Air Defence Force; operating the highly sophisticated Rapier anti-aircraft missile system in defence of the Falkland Islands. The 2004 Defence Review passes operation of the Rapier system to the Royal Artillery, hence the Squadron now provides a key operational detection capability for the protection of the UK's deployed land and air forces worldwide.

4624 (COUNTY OF OXFORD) MOVEMENTS SQUADRON

4624 Squadron's role is 'To provide Air Transport (Handling) support to allied operations worldwide'. In achieving their mission, Squadron members are trained to be responsible for the safe loading and unloading of passengers and freight to RAF and civil charter transport aircraft. The Squadron is the largest in the Reserve Air Forces and its establishment of 300 personnel represents 23% of the RAF's Movements' capability. The Squadron has deployed to Iraq and to Bosnia, Croatia and Afghanistan.

4626 (COUNTY OF WILTSHIRE) AEROMEDICAL EVACUATION SQUADRON

4626 Squadron is based at RAF Lyneham, where it provides aeromedical evacuation facilities

from deployed combat zones to hospital accommodation. Over the past 14 years, squadron personnel have flown over four million miles, undertaking peacekeeping aeromedical evacuation duties from most parts of the world. In January 2003, the Squadron was mobilised in support of Operation Telic and its personnel served in a variety of locations in the Middle East.

7006 (VR) INTELLIGENCE SQUADRON

7006 (VR) Flight is based at RAF High Wycombe and its role is to provide trained intelligence personnel to augment the RAF. Squadron personnel have supported numerous RAF operations by augmenting the MoD in London, Strike Command Headquarters at High Wycombe, NATO Headquarters in Brussels and Naples, Kuwait, the Falkland Islands, the Gulf, Cyprus and the

USA, as well as numerous UK bases.

7010 (VR) PHOTOGRAPHIC INTERPRETATION SQUADRON

7010 (VR) Squadron is based at the Headquarters Intelligence Reserves, RAF Waddington. The Squadron's current role is to provide imagery analysis support to the Joint Air Reconnaissance Intelligence Centre (JARIC) at RAF Brampton in Cambridgeshire, and to the Tactical Imagery Intelligence Wing (TIW), based at RAF Marham, in Norfolk. Analysts were deployed during Operation Telic where they interpreted imagery on a number of systems in a very short timescale in hot and challenging locations.

7630 (VR) INTELLIGENCE SQUADRON

7630 (VR) Squadron provides the RAF Humint element within the Joint

Service Intelligence Organisation at DISC Chicksands and provides a pool of linguists to assist all three Services in exercises and operations involving foreign nationals. The Squadron linguists have been used extensively in all operational theatres, particularly in the recent war in Iraq as part of the Joint Field Intelligence Team.

7644 (VR) PUBLIC RELATIONS SQUADRON

7644 (VR) Squadron provides PR support for RAF and NATO forces worldwide. In the first Gulf War, the Kosovo campaign, Sierra Leone, Afghanistan, and more recently, in Iraq, Squadron officers were deployed as advisors to senior officers as well as working in and running UK and multi-national press information centres. Now part of RAF Strike Command, the Squadron works alongside colleagues throughout the RAF and NATO.

1359 FLIGHT (HERCULES RESERVIST AIRCREW)

1359 Flight is embedded on LXX

Today's Auxiliaries

Squadron at RAF Lyneham, where they provide five Hercules 'K' crews and, in future years, four Hercules 'J' crews to augment the Hercules Force. Reservist aircrew, who train to the same standards as the Regular RAF crews, are drawn from retired RAF aircrew who served for at least one operational tour on the Hercules. Over 85% of the work completed by Hercules reservists is in direct support of the RAF Lyneham operational task.

PROVOST SQUADRON

The RAuxAF Police Squadron is based at RAF Henlow, and was established within the RAF's Tactical Provost Wing (TPW) to provide security support to the RAF air transport fleet worldwide. Their role includes searching of passengers and cargo, the guarding of aircraft and cargoes, and the assessment of airfield security. The current establishment totals 48, which includes both permanent staff and reservists. The Squadron recruits applicants without any previous experience, but approximately 30% of the Squadron's strength are former Military Police personnel. ∎

So what makes a bank clerk or a sheep farmer don a uniform at weekends and head to his nearest RAF station to train as an auxiliary? There are probably many answers. Some do it as a hobby, some feel it a duty to Queen and Country; many love the camaraderie that working as part of a close-knit team offers. Many enjoy learning new trades or skills and some feel that it assists them in personal development. However, what is certain is that every auxiliary possesses heaps of enthusiasm and it is this, more than anything, which shows through.

The RAuxAF recruits individuals from the age of 17 to 50 and no previous service experience is necessary, although many former servicemen and women do enlist. Recruits complete a two-week initial training course and then commence further training in a chosen trade. Members are required to carry out a minimum of 27 days training each year, but most do more and this can speed up training considerably. RAuxAF personnel are closely integrated with their regular counterparts as often as possible and each year they complete a two-week period of continuous training, usually on an RAF station in the UK, but sometimes overseas.

Of course, to make this all work, members need the support of their families and employers. Employers often give reservists time off work to train, recognising that their reservist skills have a place in their civilian jobs. There is legislation in place to protect an individual's civilian job if he or she is mobilised and generally, employers are very supportive. Auxiliaries' efforts are valued and whilst it is recognised that money is not the main consideration, personnel are paid for the time they spend on duty. The RAuxAF believes in the ethos of 'working hard and playing hard', so as well as the training received, opportunities exist to participate in many additional activities.

There are opportunities for volunteers to serve in many different roles and locations. Full details of the locations and the jobs carried out by reservists are described on the RAuxAF web site www.rafreserves.com. If you would like to speak to someone you may telephone our recruiting hotline on 0845 605 5555. ∎

L85 rifle. The personal weapon of all AuxAF personnel

AIR BATTLE MANAGEMENT

RAF E-3D Sentry refuelling from a USAF KC-135

3 Group's Mission is 'To generate and develop agile Intelligence, Surveillance and Reconnaissance, and Command and Battlespace Management, capabilities in support of the delivery of operational effect'.

The aircraft, equipment and personnel of Number 3 Group form the backbone of the UK's ability to understand the operational environment through the construction of a picture of air, maritime and land operations at home or overseas. The information gathered from the various 3 Group sensors supports a Commander in decision making as well as the command and control of UK and coalition assets on operations and during peacetime. Working together to achieve this task, aircraft and crews of the E3-D Sentry, the Nimrod in both MR2 and R1 variant, and the Canberra PR9 operate alongside the 3 Group Air Traffic Control and Air Surveillance and Control Systems sensors, control facilities and operators expert in tactical control. From 2006 this capability will be augmented by Sentinel R1 aircraft in the air-ground battlefield surveillance role. With the Ballistic Missile Early Warning System at RAF Fylingdales, and Space Based Infra Red Satellite systems, our surveillance capability reaches from the oceans depths to the high frontier of space.

The Group also provides a military Search and Rescue service. Utilising the Sea King Mark 3 and 3A, the crews of our yellow SAR helicopters work alongside both civilian and the five RAF Mountain Rescue Teams, providing

Sentinel R1 carrying out evaluation trials

life-saving assistance to both military personnel and civilians who find themselves in distress. This rescue force is co-ordinated by the Aeronautical Rescue and Co-ordination Centre that, when necessary, is assisted by aircraft from the Nimrod MR2 force.

Number 3 Group will disband in April 2006.

The airborne surveillance, reconnaissance and Search and Rescue forces will transfer to Number 2 Group, with the Air Traffic Control and Air Surveillance and Control systems being brought under command of the Deputy Commander-in-Chief, Headquarters Strike Command. ■

E-3D Sentry AEW1

Powerplant:
Four CFM 56 2A-3 turbofans
Thrust: 24,000lbs each
Wingspan: 44.98m
Length: 46.68m
Height: 12.7m
Max T/O weight: 151,136kg
Max endurance: 11 hours
Speed: 460kts
Ceiling: 35,000ft plus

The RAF operates seven E-3D Sentry aircraft in the airborne surveillance and command-and-control role. The aircraft are based at RAF Waddington, where they are operated by Nos 8 and 23 Squadrons as the UK's contribution to the NATO Airborne Early Warning and Control Force. The E-3D also forms one arm of the UK Intelligence, Surveillance, Target Acquisition and Reconnaissance (ISTAR) triad of Sentinel R1, E-3D and Nimrod R1 aircraft. Whilst primarily procured as an airborne early warning aircraft, the E-3D has been extensively employed in the Airborne Warning and Control System (AWACS) role. The E-3D Sentry, known to the RAF as the AEW1, is based on the commercial Boeing 707-320B aircraft, which has been extensively modified and updated to accommodate modern mission systems. Mission endurance is approximately 11 hours (over 5000nmls), although this can be extended by air-to-air refuelling. The E-3D is the only aircraft in the RAF's inventory capable of air-to-air refuelling by both the American 'flying-boom' system and the RAF's 'probe-and-drogue' method.

The normal crew complement of 18 comprises four flight-deck crew, three technicians and an 11-man mission crew. The mission crew comprises a tactical director (mission crew commander), a fighter allocator, three weapons controllers, a surveillance controller, two surveillance operators, a data-link manager, a communications operator and an electronic-support-measures operator. The Sentry's roles include air and sea surveillance, airborne command and control, weapons control and it can also operate as an extensive communications platform.

The aircraft cruises at 30,000ft and 400kts and its Northrop Grumman AN/APY-2 high-performance, multi-mode lookdown radar, housed in the black radome, is able to separate airborne and maritime targets from ground and sea clutter. One E-3D flying at 30,000ft can scan at distances of over 300nmls; it can detect low-flying targets or maritime surface contacts within 215nmls and it can detect medium-level airborne targets at ranges in excess of 280nmls. The multi-mode radar provides lookdown surveillance to the radar horizon and an electronic vertical scan of the radar beam provides target elevation and beyond-the-horizon operation for long-range surveillance of medium and high-altitude aircraft. These attributes allow it to determine the location, altitude, course and speed of large numbers of airborne targets. The aircraft's mission systems can separate, manage and display targets individually on situation displays within the aircraft, or it can transmit the information to ground-based and ship-based units using a wide variety of digital data links. ∎

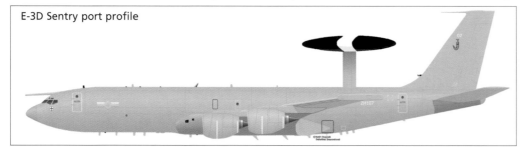

E-3D Sentry port profile

E-3D Sentry at high altitude

© John Dibbs

Powerplant:
Two RRD BR710 turbofans
Thrust:	14,750lbs each
Wingspan:	28.65m
Length:	30.3m
Height:	7.57m
Max T/O weight:	42,500kg
Endurance:	9 hours+
Speed:	Mach 0.75+
Ceiling:	40,000ft+

ASTOR (Airborne Stand-Off Radar) will provide a long-range, battlefield-intelligence, target-imaging and tracking radar for the RAF and the Army and will have surveillance applications in peacetime, wartime and in crisis operations. The prime contractor selected to provide the ASTOR system is Raytheon Systems Limited, using the Bombardier Global Express aircraft as the air platform. The system comprises three basic components, or segments. The first segment is the air platform, a modified twin-engined Global Express business jet, called the Sentinel R1 by the RAF, equipped with a radar system capable of both Synthetic Aperture Radar (SAR) and Moving Target Indicator (MTI) functions. The SAR will enable all-weather, day and night reconnaissance and surveillance to be carried out; the MTI will enable the operators to monitor the activity of mobile ground targets.

The second segment comprises two transportable Ground Stations (GS) to support deployed HQ and six mobile GS to support Division and Brigade. Each GS can receive, store and exploit radar information down-linked from the air-platform and present it, via existing communications networks, in a variety of formats to commanders, tacticians and weapons operators on the battlefield. Finally, the support segment provides important mission-support functionality, such as mission planning and mission data replay, at the main operating base (RAF Waddington) and for deployed operations. A two pilot flight-deck crew will operate the aircraft, with a mission crew nominally comprising a mission controller and two image analysts. The aircraft, currently in production as an ultra-long range business jet, will be modified to include a radome under the forward fuselage to house the radar and datalink antennae, and a radome on the upper fuselage to house the SATCOM antenna. The aircraft will operate at altitudes in excess of 40,000ft with a mission endurance over 9 hours.

The engines used by the ASTOR aircraft are the Rolls-Royce Deutschland (RRD) BR710 engines, which are very similar to those used on the Nimrod MRA4 maritime patrol aircraft. Defensive aids will include a radar-warning receiver, a missile warning system, a towed radar decoy and

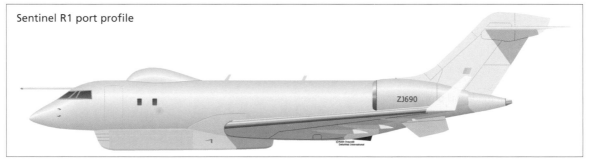

Sentinel R1 port profile

ZJ690

Sentinel R1 at high level

chaff and flare dispensers. The radar is an upgraded version of the Raytheon ASARS-2 radar used on the U-2 aircraft and will be capable of providing high resolution images of the battlefield at ranges of several hundred kilometres. The SAR mode will provide high quality radar images of the area surveyed, while the MTI mode will detect moving vehicles operating in the area. The SAR can be operated in spot mode to produce high-resolution imagery over relatively small areas of fixed location. The SAR swath mode can collect lower-resolution imagery broadside to the aircraft as it proceeds but at a much greater width than SAR spot. Multiple passes using SAR swath mode can effectively provide wide area surveillance of fixed and static targets. These images can be exploited by the airborne mission crew, or down-linked from the aircraft in near real time to the ASTOR GS, to generate intelligence reports for commanders.

It is currently envisaged that ASTOR will begin to enter service from the end of 2006, when it will become the most advanced long range, airborne-surveillance system of its kind in the world. Five Sentinel R1 aircraft will be purchased and operated by No 5(AC) Squadron, based at RAF Waddington, where they will form one arm of the surveillance triad of Sentinel R1, E-3D Sentry and Nimrod R1. ■

Powerplant:

	Four Rolls-Royce Spey
	251 tubofans
Thrust:	12,140lbs each
Wingspan:	35m
Length:	35.86m
Height:	9.14m
Max T/O weight:	83,636kg
Internal Fuel:	38,182kg
Endurance:	10hrs
Speed:	360kts
Ceiling:	44,000ft

The Nimrod R1 is a derivative of the Nimrod MR2 maritime patrol aircraft and is operated by No 51 Squadron, from RAF Waddington. The Nimrod R1 has a highly sophisticated and sensitive suite of systems used for reconnaissance and gathering electronic intelligence. The ability of the Nimrod to transit at high speed and then loiter in an operational area at lower speed for long periods makes it ideally suited to the task. Air refuelling can extend the Nimrod R1's endurance should the task demand.

The Nimrod R1 is operated by a four-man flight deck crew of two pilots, a flight engineer and a weapon systems officer, and an electronic reconnaissance crew of 24 reconnaissance-equipment operators commanded by a mission supervisor. The aircraft is fitted with two inertial navigation systems and a satellite-based global positioning system to assist in the requirement for accurate navigation.

The Nimrod R1 can be distinguished from the maritime MR2 aircraft by the absence of the tail-mounted Magnetic Anomaly Detector boom. ■

The Nimrod R1 can be refuelled in mid-air by the probe mounted above the cockpit

The sensor operators and mission supervisor work at consoles in the fuselage

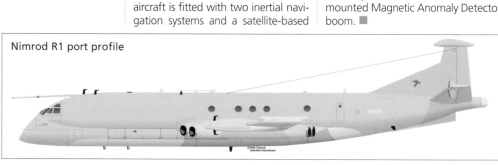

Nimrod R1 port profile

A plan view of an R1

Canberra PR9 Photographic and electro-optical reconnaissance

Powerplant:

Two Rolls-Royce Avon Mk
206 turbofans
Thrust: 11,250lbs each
Wing span: 20.66m
Length: 20.36m
Height: 4.75m
Max T/O weight: 24,227kg
Speed: 450kts
Ceiling: 48,000ft

Number 39 (1 PRU) Squadron is the only remaining Canberra squadron in service with the RAF and is based at RAF Marham, in Norfolk. Its role in peacetime is photographic and electro-optical reconnaissance, strategic air reconnaissance to meet overseas intelligence requirements, aerial surveys within the UK and overseas, and occasional low-level tasks. In transition to war, the role becomes medium-level, high-level and long-range oblique imagery capture in support of UK or Coalition Operations. To achieve its task, the Squadron operates four Canberra PR9 (Photographic Reconnaissance) aircraft. The PR9 was the final development of the Canberra airframe and first entered service with No 39 Squadron in October 1962. Sensors and navigation equipment have since been updated, but the engines and airframe remain essentially the same.

Currently, the aircraft sensor-fit includes a survey camera, a panoramic camera and a long-range electro-optical camera. The survey camera is used mainly to produce vertical images on 9-inch square negatives for mapping purposes. The panoramic camera, which can be directed to any position from the horizon to the vertical, produces a swathe of negatives giving an oblique image of a target. The electro-optical camera can produce only oblique images, but the imagery can be highly magnified and transmitted to ground stations via an on-board datalink. In addition to the sensor platform updates, the PR9 has a much-enhanced navigation suite and, to improve survival in operational theatres, it has been fitted with a Skyguardian Radar Warning Receiver, and an Electronic Protective Measures suite, which dispenses chaff and infrared decoy flares from packs mounted internally in the underside of the wings. During its earlier life, the PR9 had a low-level and medium-level night reconnaissance role using Infrared Line Scan equipment, but its current role is restricted to daytime reconnaissance.

With a pilot and weapon systems officer crew, the aircraft regularly operates at heights above 40,000ft and can remain airborne for up to 4½ hours, although it cannot be refuelled in the air. The Squadron recently saw operational service over Afghanistan and Iraq and has continued to provide surveillance and survey imagery of Kosovo and the Balkans over the last six years. After exemplary service for over 40 years, the PR9 will finally be withdrawn from service in July 2006. ■

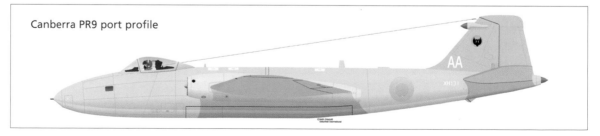

Canberra PR9 port profile

Canberra PR9 conducting a high-level aerial survey

Nimrod MR2

Powerplant:

	Four Rolls-Royce Spey 250 turbofans
Thrust:	12,500lbs each
Wingspan:	35m
Length:	38.65m
Height:	9.14m
Max T/O weight:	83,636kg
Internal fuel:	38,182kg
Endurance:	9.5hrs
Speed:	360kts
Ceiling:	44,000ft

Weapons:	Sting Ray Harpoon

The Nimrod MR1 entered service in 1969 and was upgraded to MR2 standard in the late 1970s. While the flight deck and general systems remained the same, the Mission System was given a significant upgrade. The Nimrod is the only jet powered maritime patrol aircraft in military service and offers the advantages of speed and height in transit, while still capable of operating for long on-task periods.

The Nimrod is used in four main roles: Anti Submarine Warfare (ASW), Anti-Surface-Unit Warfare (ASUW), Intelligence and Communications Support and Search and Rescue (SAR). The operating crew comprises two pilots and a flight engineer, two weapon systems officers (WSO) (tactical and routine), and a WSO who is the sensor and communications coordinator. He is, in turn, supported by a team of two 'wet' weapon systems operators (WSOps) and four 'dry' WSOps. The 'wet' team supervise the aircraft's acoustic processors, which monitor active and passive sonobuoys, whilst the 'dry' team manage a range of radar and non-acoustic sensors, all of which are essential to delivering Nimrod's full capability. The aircraft can carry in excess of 200 sonobuoys internally, of several different types, both active and passive, which are delivered via two unpressurised 6-buoy rotary launchers and two pressurised singleshot launchers. The Nimrod's offensive weapons include Sting Ray torpedoes for use in the ASW and ASUW role and for self-defence the aircraft is fitted with Defensive Aids systems and may be armed with four wing-mounted Sidewinder air-to-air missiles. For SAR purposes the aircraft has a selection of air deliverable, multi-seat dinghies and survival packs.

The majority of the Nimrod's tasking comes from the UK Maritime Air Ops Centre at the Joint Northwood HQ. Peacetime work includes worldwide surface and sub-surface surveillance and the maintenance of a permanent standby for UK and overseas operations or SAR in support of the Aeronautical Rescue Coordination Centre, collocated at RAF Kinloss. SAR tasks include long-range search and shepherd, assistance to SAR helicopters and coordination of search activities as the On-Scene Commander at major incidents. The aircraft routinely operates over the sea down to 200 feet, but is limited to 300 feet at night or in bad weather.

The Nimrod MR2 has also provided a continual presence in the Middle East since late 2001. In that time, employment of the aircraft has evolved to take on an additional range of non-traditional tasks, including overland Electro-Optic IMINT (Image Intelligence) surveillance of Iraq and Afghanistan, and IMINT and communications support to coalition ground troops. The Nimrod MR2 will continue in service until it is replaced by the MRA4, which is expected to enter service around 2011. ∎

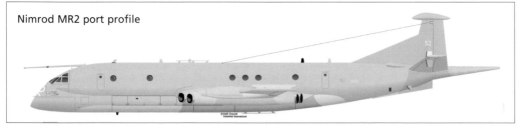

Nimrod MR2 port profile

A Nimrod MR2 just prior to lift-off

Nimrod MRA4

Powerplant:

Four RRD BR710 turbofans
Thrust:	14,900lbs each
Wingspan:	38.71m
Length:	38.63m
Height:	9.14m
Max T/O weight:	105,075kg
Internal fuel:	38,182kg
Endurance:	15hrs
Speed:	520kts
Ceiling:	42,000ft

Weapons: Sting Ray

The Nimrod MRA4 is expected to start entering service with the RAF at around the turn of the decade when it will replace the present MR2, which first entered service in the early 1980s. Although the MRA4 looks similar to the MR2, only the basic fuselage shell and the tail is shared between the two aircraft and the MRA4 will have completely new systems and a new, longer wing carrying advanced Rolls-Royce Deutschland (RRD) BR710 turbofan engines. The engines are 30% more fuel-efficient and 25% more powerful than the Rolls-Royce Spey 250 engines they replace. The aircraft's maximum weight has increased from around 87

The ultra-modern console suite on the MRA4

tonnes to approximately 104 tonnes and it can fly for longer periods than its predecessor with a bigger payload in both weapons and sensors. The Nimrod MRA4 will have a multi-tasking role, which will include its main roles of anti-submarine warfare, anti-surface-unit warfare, maritime reconnaissance, search and rescue and ISTAR but, in addition, it will be used in law-enforcement tasks including anti-smuggling and anti-gun-running operations, fisheries protection and counter-terrorism duties.

The MRA4 operating crew will consist of two pilots and eight mission crew members operating new state-of-the-art radar, electro-optic and acoustic sensor systems. The new flight deck is an all-glass cockpit, which incorporates many of the systems, displays and integrated avionics developed for the Airbus series of civil airliners. There are a total of seven liquid-crystal, full-colour displays – the seventh display presents tactical information fed from the sensors for use by the pilots. The aircraft navigation system incorporates an interfaced navigation computer and flight management computer, which automatically controls the aircraft using two laser inertial navigation system and

two global-positioning systems.

The heart of the mission system is the entirely new Tactical Command System, which is based around the seven reconfigurable, high-resolution, multi-function colour display workstations used by the mission crew, plus the pilots' tactical display. The primary sensor will be the Thales Searchwater 2000MR multi-mode search radar. This is a new, extremely high-performance radar designed for all-weather operation and optimised to have a high probability of tracking small targets in poor weather. It can automatically track a large number of surface contacts. Other sensors include electronic support measures, an acoustic detection system, magnetic anomaly detection equipment and an electro-optical surveillance and detection system. A new defensive-aids system will include a radar warning receiver, a missile approach receiver and integral chaff/flare dispensers.

The MRA4 will carry an extensive range of weapons and sensors in the weapons bay. Weapons management will be conducted via a stores management system, which carries out inventory tracking control, air-to-air and air-to-sea weapon control, and built-in test and fault diagnostic systems. ∎

The high-technology cockpit of the Nimrod MRA4 is a world away from the cramped dial-based flightdeck of the original type

Harpoon Autonomous, over-the-horizon, all-weather, anti-ship

Anti-ship missile

Length:	3.8m
Weight:	527kg
Range:	68nmls
Guidance:	Inertial mid-course/Terminal active radar
Aircraft:	Nimrod MR2

The Harpoon AGM-84D, produced by McDonnell Aircraft and Missile Systems, a subsidiary of the Boeing Company, is a fully autonomous, over-the-horizon, all-weather, anti-ship missile, designed as a high-subsonic, sea-skimming weapon. Operated by the Nimrod MR2 and MRA4, the missile is pre-programmed with targeting information and then launched from the aircraft to fly to the target using its integral turbojet motor. To operate autonomously, the Harpoon is equipped with an active Phase J-band radar for terminal acquisition of the target, combined with a radar altimeter and a digital mid-course guidance system. The Harpoon can be launched at long range from its intended target, thereby minimising the danger of counter-detection and subsequent attack against the launch aircraft.

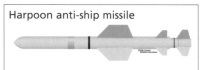

Harpoon anti-ship missile

The missile is made up of four main components: the guidance section, the warhead, the sustainer section and the boat-tail assembly. The guidance section contains the radar seeker and radar altimeter, which are integrated with the missile guidance unit to maintain the missile on its programmed flight profile and guide it to its target. The sustainer section contains the jet engine to power the missile during sustained flight. The boat-tail assembly contains four electro-mechanical actuators, which operate four external fins at the rear of the missile to control the missile's direction

during flight. The missile also carries mid-line fins, which are attached to the sustainer section, but these are used solely to provide lift during flight. The warhead, weighing some 222kg (489lbs), is a high-explosive unit capable of surviving the initial impact with the target's hull, enabling the missile to detonate inside the ship, so increasing its destructive effectiveness.

The Harpoon has proved to be both exceptionally reliable and extremely effective. Its low-level, high-speed attack profile, coupled with its high resistance to countermeasures, make it an excellent anti-ship weapon. Operational use in the Gulf War showed that, once the missile's terminal radar-seeker had acquired its target, the missile achieved a 100% success rate and caused maximum damage to the target ships. ■

Harpoon at low-level, on its way to a target vessel

An artist's impression of a Nimrod launching a Harpoon

Length:	2.6m
Diameter:	0.354m
Weight:	265kg
Max depth:	Below 760 metres
Speed:	Over 40kts
Warhead:	29kg shaped charge
Aircraft:	Nimrod MR2 Nimrod MRA4

The Sting Ray is a lightweight, air-launched, electrically-powered, homing torpedo carried by the Nimrod MR2 and MRA4 for use against either deep ocean or coastal water submarine targets. It is powered by a seawater battery, and combines low-noise and excellent manoeuvrability with a high-speed attack capability. The Sting Ray is an autonomous weapon which, having received pre-launch, search pattern information from the launch aircraft, uses its active sonar and tactical software to search for, localise and attack its submarine target. The Sting Ray's in-built, tactical software enables it to deal with complex countermeasure defence scenarios used by its target.

After being launched, the torpedo descends by parachute until it enters the water. The torpedo then activates its propulsion system, which discards the parachute and carries out an immediate check to determine the

A Sting Ray lightweight torpedo, after release and prior to entry into the water

water depth. If the water is shallow, the torpedo runs at a fixed height following the contours of the sea bed. The torpedo's on-board computer, which controls the acoustics and the homing and attack profile, carries out a search pattern based upon the pre-launch inputs of safety ceiling, initial search depth, magnetic variation and torpedo heading, until the target has been acquired. The target is classified and identified from the return signals and, once acquired, the torpedo starts homing onto it. The torpedo is able to

determine the target's speed, heading and depth, thus enabling the weapon to select the best attack profile and optimum impact angle to ensure the torpedo's shaped charge works to maximum effect when penetrating a submarine's hull. Should the Sting Ray miss its target, it has the ability to turn and home in again for another attack. The current version of the Sting Ray torpedo, designated Mod 0, is receiving a major performance upgrade. The new version will enter service with the RAF as Mod 1. ■

Sting Ray torpedo

BMEWS RAF Fylingdales

The Solid State Phased Array Radar (AN/FPS 126) is located at RAF Fylingdales, North Yorkshire. The Unit was originally established in 1963 as one of three sites which formed the US Ballistic Missile Early Warning System (BMEWS). The iconic 'golf balls' that dominated the site for over 30 years housed large mechanical tracking radars; these were replaced in 1992 by the Solid State Phased Array Radar (SSPAR). The radar's primary function is to provide missile warning data to Headquarters RAF Strike Command and Cheyenne Mountain Operations Center, Colorado – the home of North American Aerospace Defense Command or NORAD. The radar also has a secondary mission of space surveillance. Although the SSPAR is manned and operated by RAF personnel, operational command and control is shared jointly between the UK and US in accordance with a bilateral government agreement.

The SSPAR works in the frequency range 420-450 MHz (B-band) utilising linear frequency modulated chirped pulses for both surveillance and tracking functions. Housed within a single truncated pyramid, it is the only 3-faced phased array radar in existence. Each aerial face is approximately 25.6m in diameter and is comprised of 2560 active antenna elements that produce a peak power output of 2.6 MW across the three faces. The radar has a maximum range of 3000nm and produces a permanent surveillance fence through 360°. Any object that penetrates the surveillance fence will trigger the radar's threat processing software, which calculates

The active antennae of the SSPAR

whether the object is an incoming missile or an orbiting spacecraft. For missile objects, the radar will present launch and impact location information to the operator. The operator has only 60 seconds to determine the validity of the event before upward reporting to UK and US commands. The radar is capable of tracking up to 800 missile objects simultaneously.

The SSPAR is currently being upgraded under the Upgrade Early Warning Radar (UEWR) Programme. This programme, due for completion by the end of 2006, will enhance the radar's tracking capability to enable the production of highly accurate missile flight data. This data will be used by a US Ballistic Missile Defence System that is designed

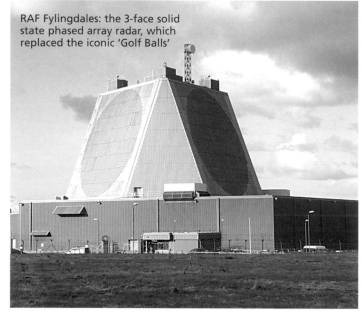

RAF Fylingdales: the 3-face solid state phased array radar, which replaced the iconic 'Golf Balls'

to intercept incoming ballistic missile attacks against North America.

Although missile warning is the radar's primary task, the secondary task of space surveillance accounts for approximately 98% of the Unit's output. As part of a global space surveillance network, RAF Fylingdales is tasked to detect, track, identify and catalogue all man-made objects in earth orbit. There are currently over 9,600 man-made objects orbiting the planet, over two thirds of which are space debris. Over 28,000 objects have been catalogued since the first space launch in 1957. On a daily basis, the radar tracks over 4000 space objects and provides updated orbital information on each object to the Space Control Center, in Colorado, who maintain the definitive satellite catalogue. RAF Fylingdales tracks objects that range in size from 10cm^2 up to the largest man-made object in orbit, which is currently the International Space Station. The Unit is also the first radar sensor to track space shuttle launches on their initial orbits.

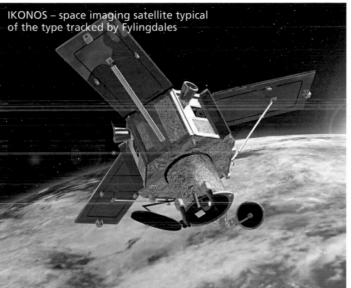

IKONOS – space imaging satellite typical of the type tracked by Fylingdales

Today's military operations are vulnerable to various means of foreign intelligence collection, including the use of orbiting satellites to produce imagery and electronic intelligence data. RAF Fylingdales has an additional national task of providing a Satellite Warning Service to UK forces. The Service uses orbital data to produce overflight warn-ing of potentially hostile intelli-gence-gathering satellites, there-by enabling UK forces to conceal or suspend any sensitive activities to prevent compromise. With recent advances in technology, commercial satellite imagery is now widely available over the Internet; this imagery also poses a potential threat to military operations.

With the increased military reliance on Space based assets in the Intelligence, Surveillance, Target Acquisition and Reconnaissance (ISTAR) role, much of RAF Fylingdale's daily work is involved with the provi-sion of information to command-ers at all levels of the potential threat to operational security brought about by the 'eyes and ears in space'. Information about satellites, which are positioned to observe locations of strategic or operational importance is passed to the UK intelligence services, other government agencies and military commanders in order that appropriate measures may be taken.

Operating 24 hours per day, RAF Fylingdales has been provid-ing vital missile warning and space surveillance data to UK and US commands for over 40 years. Despite the cessation of the Cold War, the rapid prolifer-ation of ballistic missile technolo-gy and the dramatic increase in global space activity have rein-forced the strategic significance of the Unit well into the 21st century. ■

Since the end of the Cold War, the UK's areas of military interest have expanded to the extent that air power is now deployed on a global basis. But to allow air power to deploy rapidly, Joint Commanders must be able to call upon air and space-based sensor systems to provide specific intelligence on particular areas of interest. The more dispersed, less defined battlespace makes global surveillance using space-based systems an invaluable and increasingly indispensable tool in the conduct of modern operations. The expense of 'big space' (large, expensive satellites) is being overcome by the commercially driven development of much smaller, more affordable satellites. Small satellites (some as small as a drinks can) are already being used, merging commercial off-the-shelf technology with innovative control techniques. Few nations can afford multi-million pound large satellites, but small satellites can be built and launched for a fraction of the time and cost and used in conjunction with commercially available space-based services. In addition, small satellites offer greater operational flexibility and the gap between their capability and that of the traditional 'big space' satellites is rapidly closing. Consequently, space capability could be an operational asset rather than a strategic one, limited to a few space-capable countries. Commanders could call on responsive, gap-filling communications and novel space-based surveillance capabilities, such as wide-area coverage, multi-spectral

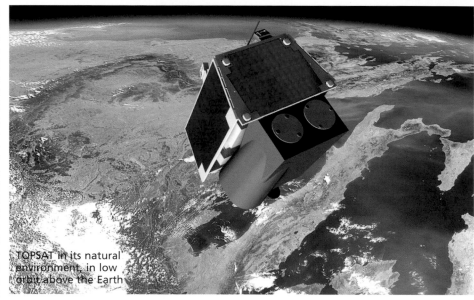

TOPSAT in its natural environment, in low orbit above the Earth

imaging and change detection techniques, to help visualise the battlespace and provide situational awareness to aid decision-making. Small satellites offer affordable access to space for the UK and pave the way for persistent, space-based contribution to the Intelligence, Surveillance and Reconnaissance capability mix. Space is no longer the sole domain of a few nations and to demonstrate this, in August 2005, the UK launched a small satellite (Technology Demonstrator) called TOPSAT

from the Russian Cosmodrome in Plesetsk. This is a jointly funded project by the MoD and the British National Space Centre. TOPSAT is an enhanced imaging microsatellite with a mobile ground station to download data in near real-time that can be processed and displayed to deployed forces. The small satellite potential demonstrated by TOPSAT allows the UK to work alongside its US, NATO and other partners to exploit the ultimate high ground of space, free from any overflight restrictions. ■

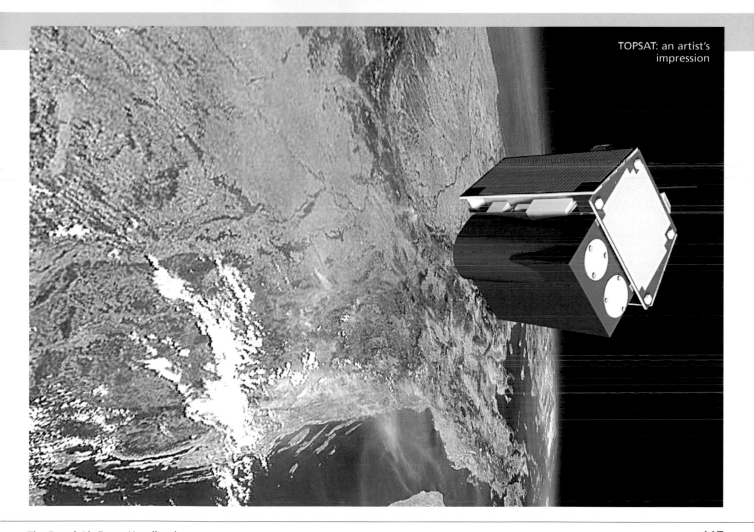

TOPSAT: an artist's impression

MQ-1 Predator UAV

The RAF's Predator unit, 1115 Flight, was formed on 28 January 2005 and comprises 45 British personnel who have been specially selected from a tri-service background. They are attached to the USAF and are fully embedded into the USAF Predator squadrons. The main UAV operated by 1115 Flight and their USAF partners is the MQ-1 Predator, which is a medium-altitude, long-endurance, remotely piloted aircraft. The MQ-1's primary role is reconnaissance, but it has the additional capability to strike against ground targets. The Predator's role is to provide real-time video imagery to ground commanders during Operation Iraqi Freedom and Operation Enduring Freedom (Afghanistan).

Although Predator is primarily an Intelligence Surveillance and Reconnaissance (ISR) platform, it is also equipped with two Hellfire anti-tank missiles and can be used to strike vehicles, personnel and small buildings. The aircraft is equipped with a colour nose camera (generally used by the pilot for flight control), a day variable-aperture TV camera, and a variable-aperture infrared camera for low-light/night operations. The MQ-1 Predator carries the Multi-spectral Targeting System (MTS), which integrates electro-optical and infrared sensors, a laser designator and a laser illuminator into a single sensor payload. Command users who are able to receive Predator's downlink are able to task the pay-load operator in real time for images or video. The MTS laser designator is used to guide its Hellfire missiles, whilst the laser marker can be used to identify targets to troops on the ground equipped with night-vision goggles. The basic operating crew for the Predator is one pilot and a sensor operator.

The crew fly the Predator from inside the Ground Control Station (GCS) and control the aircraft via the Ground Data Terminal (GDT) antenna, which provides line-of-sight communications for take off and landing, or via the Predator Primary Satellite Link (PPSL), which provides over-the-horizon communications for the aircraft. The aircraft includes a VHF radio which can be relayed via satellite, an Identification Friend or Foe with Mode 4, an upgraded turbo-charged engine and glycol-weeping 'wet wings' for ice mitigation, fuel injection, longer wings and dual alternators. The aircraft is 8.23m long and has a 16.15m wing span.

The system was originally designed with three major components: four aircraft, a GCS and

Satellite links are a major part of Predator control systems

1115 Flt personnel preparing a Predator for flight

a PPSL. The system is supported by approximately 55 personnel for deployed 24/7 worldwide operations. The Predator aircraft can be disassembled and, along with the GCS, is transportable in a Hercules C-130 (or larger) transport aircraft. The Predator can operate from a 1524m by 23m hard surface runway.

An alternative method of employment, Remote Split Operations, employs a smaller version of the GCS called the Launch and Recovery GCS (LRGCS). The crew in the LRGCS conduct take off and landing operations at the forward deployed location and once the aircraft is airborne and flying at approximately 5000ft a GCS based at Nellis AFB, in Nevada, will take control via satellite links and conduct the mission. On completion, the Nellis crew will hand the Predator back to the deployed crew who will land the aircraft using line-of-sight C band communications.

At present there are three Predator Squadrons operated by the USAF, one reconnaissance and training squadron and two operational squadrons. ■

Powerplant

Two Rolls-Royce Gnome turboshafts	
Thrust:	2778shp combined
Length:	22.15m
Fuselage length:	14.4m
Width:	4.98m
Height:	5.13m
Rotor span:	18.90m
Max T/O weight:	9705kg
Speed:	125kts
Ceiling:	10,000ft

The Westland Sea King HAR3 entered RAF service in 1978 and the 3A in 1996; both marks of aircraft are used in the Search and Rescue (SAR) role. The aircraft are operated from six locations around the UK, with each location supporting two aircraft. There is also a detachment of two HAR3s providing SAR cover in the Falkland Islands. The SAR squadrons provide 24-hour cover around the UK and the Falkland Islands throughout each year. Each squadron maintains a 15-minutes readiness state during daylight hours and a 45-minutes readiness state during the hours of darkness.

For the search aspect of its role, the Sea King is able to operate to precise navigational standards and is fitted with a multi-band homing system,

RAF Sea Kings are painted a high-visibility yellow paint scheme

satellite navigation systems, a search radar, a comprehensive avionics suite and a large selection of radios. For its rescue role, the aircraft is equipped with a hydraulically-operated main rescue hoist, an electrically-operated

emergency rescue hoist and electrical connections suitable for powering medical equipment such as incubators. The SAR fleet of Sea Kings are fitted with a video/infrared detection pod, which is similar to the equipment used by police helicopters, to help search for casualties. All SAR crews are trained to operate using night-vision goggles over unfamiliar terrain. The standard SAR crew is made up of four members: two pilots, one of whom is the aircraft captain, a radar operator who acts as the winch operator at the rescue scene and a winchman, normally trained to paramedic standard, who will supply immediate first-aid and recovery services at the rescue site. ■

Sea King HAR3 port profile

SAR helicopters frequently work in tandem with RNLI assets

47-003

Powerplant

	Two Pratt & Whitney
	PT6T- 3D turboshafts
Thrust:	1800shp combined
Length:	17.11m
Fuselage Length:	12.7m
Height:	3.48m
Rotor Diameter:	14.02m
Max T/O weight:	5409kg
Speed:	140kts
Ceiling:	20,000ft

The Griffin HAR2 is used as a multirole helicopter by 84 Squadron at RAF Akrotiri, Cyprus. The Squadron operates four aircraft, supplied and maintained by the civilian company FBH services, but operated by experienced military aircrews. The Griffin HAR2 is a twin-engined helicopter derived from the civilian Bell Textron 412EP helicopter and is powered by two Pratt and Whitney turboshafts rated at 1800shp. The aircraft has an advanced, composite material, four-blade main rotor system, and pendulum dampers on the rotor hub to reduce vibrations at higher cruise speeds. The composite main-blades can be interchanged and folded easily for storage. The Griffin is used by 84 Squadron for Search and Rescue duties over land in mountainous terrain during the day, and over the sea at night by using night vision goggles and its FLIR/TV turret. The Squadron's primary role is the rescue of downed aircrew in the water or on cliffs, and the rescue of personnel from military and commercial shipping.

The electrical hoist will lift three personnel and the cabin will accommodate two stretcher casualties. With full life-support equipment available in the cabin, the paramedic-trained

Griffin HAR2, with winchman in the doorway

winchmen can provide the highest level of patient care en-route to hospital. 84 Squadron operate throughout the Eastern Mediterranean area and provide great assistance to the civil communities in the region. They also support military exercises as far afield as Jordan. In the SH role, the Griffin HAR2 carries six (eight if operationally essential) fully equipped troops from the smallest and dustiest of sites, and in the VIP role it routinely carries visitors around Cyprus. The Griffin is used extensively on fire-fighting duties during the dry Cypriot summers, quelling the numerous bush fires by use of a Bambi bucket on the Under Slung Load hook. The bucket can pick up

2000lb of water and deliver it very accurately onto the seat of the fire.

The aircraft is equipped with a modern avionics suite which is fully IFR compliant and which couples to a four axis duplex autopilot. The Griffin's radar is used for weather avoidance and as a shipping search radar when operating over the sea. The aircraft has a 2hr 45mins endurance, a 120 knot cruise speed and a 3000lb payload. 84 Squadron has a total of 15 aircrew to maintain their 24/7 role. Six pilots operate in the single pilot role, whilst a total of nine WSOs share the search, rescue and paramedic duties when operating on SAR missions. ■

Griffin in the hover, winching
a casualty on board

Mountain Rescue Teams

Originally formed during the Second World War to go to the aid of crashed aircrew, the RAF Mountain Rescue Service (MRS) is now an integral part of the RAF Search and Rescue (SAR) organisation and is a volunteer force manned by servicemen and women drawn from all ranks and trades in the RAF. The MRS comprises four operational Mountain Rescue Teams (MRTs) based at RAF stations Kinloss, Leeming, Leuchars and Valley and the MRS HQ Flight, which is collocated with the MRT at RAF Valley. The MRS works closely with SAR helicopters, civilian Mountain Rescue Teams and Police, Fire and Ambulance Services and although established to aid pilots and passengers of aircraft that have crashed or force-landed in the upland regions of the UK, most callouts today are for injured or missing climbers and walkers.

Each MRT consists of eight full time staff, who look after training, equipment and administration, and 28 volunteers from the parenting

A SAR helicopter is guided in with the use of red flares

station who make up the main body of the team. The MRS is also established for up to four Search and Rescue Dog Association (SARDA) teams. Each team is required to maintain an operational team at one-hour readiness to move during the working week, but during weekend and grant periods they can reduce their readiness to conduct operational training. An operational team consists of 10 appropriately qualified personnel with the necessary specialist equipment and vehicles. The MRT deploys on exercise each weekend and public holidays (including Christmas), and members are expected to attend a minimum of two weekend exercises every month and a training briefing once a week. As well as being part of a highly trained and dedicated group, their commitment (and that of wives and girlfriends!) is reciprocated by the excellent team spirit and 'family' atmosphere that exists within the teams.

Weekend exercises usually consist of walking and climbing, with various rescue techniques and Immediate and Emergency Care training being regularly practised in addition to general mountaineering skills. No pre-requisites are required of volunteers; all that is asked is that they are willing to try hard and 'keep smiling'. The more experienced members of the team provide instruction in navigation, climbing and rescue and first aid in a training programme that begins the day a new member joins the team. From raw recruit to expert

MRTs must be prepared for all terrains and weather conditions

mountain rescuer takes about five years of continuous training and commitment.

Each MRT has its own dedicated area of responsibility; for example RAF Leuchars' MRT area lies between the English/Scottish border and a line drawn between Aberdeen and Oban; however, they are often required to operate and train outside this theoretical boundary. As the team is constantly available for callouts it operates as a self-contained unit, able to react at the required one-hour notice, day or night, and remain self-sufficient for up to thirty-six hours. During exercises they are normally based in a local village hall. Accommodation is basic – the teams often sleep on the floor (on mats!) in sleeping bags, and take turns to cook for the other members. Membership of a MRT can be very rewarding and members generally enjoy a 'work hard, play hard' lifestyle. ■

MRTs form an important part of the RAF's SAR remit

JOINT HELICOPTER COMMAND

British Army soldiers exit from
the rear ramp of an RAF Chinook

The Royal Air Force Handbook

Joint Helicopter Command

The Joint Helicopter Command (JHC) was established as a formation within Land Command in 1999 to bring together all battlefield helicopters (BH) under one organisation. Its purpose is to deliver and sustain effective BH and Air Assault Assets, operationally capable under all environmental conditions, to support the UK's Defence Mission and tasks.

The RAF Support Helicopter Force

The RAF Support Helicopter Force consists of over 3,700 RAF personnel including over 150 volunteers of the Royal Auxiliary Air Force. In generating Chinook, Puma and Merlin helicopters for operations, the RAF Support Helicopter Force provides a critical element of the JHC's BH capability. Our personnel operate and sustain our 97 RAF Support Helicopters from four bases at RAF Aldergrove in Northern Ireland, RAF Benson in Oxfordshire, RAF Odiham in Hampshire and RAF Stafford in Staffordshire.

The Changing Role of Support Helicopters

The Support Helicopter role has evolved significantly since the 1990s. During the Cold War era, Support Helicopters were mostly constrained to supporting operations behind our own lines, taking troops and supplies to the front and returning with casualties. In the modern era of expeditionary and manoeuvre warfare, the Support Helicopter Force is more frequently required to support all areas of the battlefield. The imperative for Air Manoeuvre has

led to the acquisition of new equipment that enables our aircraft to operate on deeper operations where the threat is greater.

New Equipment

Deep operations are facilitated by the deployment of Forward Arming and Refuelling Points and the use of extended-range fuel tanks. Future capabilities may include in-flight refuelling. Equally significant is the expansion in capability of night-vision equipment. The tactical advantage that night operations bring has driven the development of night-vision goggles, forward looking infra-red (FLIR) and improved cockpit and navigation systems. This has reduced the workload during night operations and allowed crews to approach a true day and night all-weather capability. Greater involvement in combined operations has also brought in new equipment that enhances our ability to operate with coalition partners.

A New Role: Joint Personnel Recovery

The Joint Personnel Recovery role is being explored by 28(AC) Squadron flying the Merlin HC3. The Merlin's digital cockpit, moving map displays, FLIR and latest generation of defensive systems will allow the aircrew to transport RAF Regiment Ground Extraction Forces and Tactical Medical Wing paramedics thorough hostile airspace to rescue isolated personnel.

The Future

The July 2004 Supplement to the Defence White Paper announced that MoD plans to invest in Future Rotorcraft Capability (FRC) to replace and enhance our existing helicopters. There is approximately £4 billion available over the next ten years, as well as further funds set aside in the next decade, which will be focused on the key capability areas of lift, reconnaissance and attack, and which will be central to future expeditionary operations. ■

Powerplant

	Two Textron Lycoming T55-L712F turboshafts
Thrust:	3750shp each
Length:	30.18m
Fuselage length:	15.54m
Height:	5.78m
Rotor diameter:	18.29m
Endurance:	2¾hrs
Max T/O weight:	24,500kg
Speed	160kts
Ceiling:	15,000ft

The RAF operates the largest fleet of Chinook Support Helicopters after the US Army, with a total of 34 HC2s, 6 HC2As and 8 HC3s (the HC3 has yet to enter operational service). The Chinook Wing, which forms the heavy-lift element of the Joint Helicopter Command (JHC), is based at RAF Odiham in Hampshire. Odiham supports three operational squadrons, No 7 Squadron, No 18 Squadron and No 27 Squadron, and the Operational Conversion Flight.

The HC2 and HC2A aircraft are used primarily for trooping and for carrying internal and/or underslung loads and can carry up to 55 troops or 10 tonnes of freight. The cabin is large enough to accommodate two Land Rovers, while the three underslung load hooks allow a huge flexibility in the type and number of loads that can be carried externally. Secondary roles include search and rescue and casualty evacuation, in which role a total of 24 stretchers can be carried. The crew consists of either two pilots, or a pilot and a weapon systems officer (WSO), and two air loadmasters. The pilot captain is responsible for the safe operation of the aircraft and completion of the mission, while the co-pilot or WSO operates the mission-management systems, navigation, communications and the self-defence suite. In the cabin are two air loadmasters who are responsible for passenger safety, load or cargo restraint, weapons operation and voice marshalling of the aircraft.

The aircraft are well equipped for their varied roles and are fitted with a satellite Global Positioning System, an Instrument Landing System, compre-

Chinook port profile

hensive avionics that enable them to fly in airways, and an extensive radio suite. The aircraft cockpit has a full night-time capability when operated with night-vision goggles, thus allowing low-level night operations in a hostile environment. The aircraft also carries dual mode landing lights that can be switched between white and infrared light, which are supported by infrared searchlights operated by the two crewmen. The Chinook is well equipped with defensive aids and has a Radar Warning Receiver, an Ultraviolet and Doppler Missile Approach Warning System, infrared jammers and chaff and flare dispensers, which can be manually or automatically fired. The aircraft can be armed with two M134 six-barrelled Miniguns, one in each front side window, and an M60D machine gun on the ramp.

The Chinook is a very capable and versatile support helicopter that can be operated in many diverse environments ranging from cold weather 'arctic' conditions to desert warfare operations. It has been involved in most of the recent UK operations such as the Falklands Conflict, Northern Ireland, the Gulf War, peace keeping in Bosnia, Kosovo operations, evacuation of Sierra Leone, operations in Afghanistan and, more recently, in Iraq. ■

AN RAF Chinook operating in the littoral environment

Powerplant

Three Rolls-Royce Turbomeca RTM 322 turbines	
Thrust:	2263shp each
Length:	22.8m
Fuselage length:	19.43m
Height:	6.62m
Rotor diameter:	18.6m
Max T/O weight:	14,600kg
Endurance:	4 hrs
Speed:	167kts
Ceiling:	15,000ft

The Merlin HC3 is operated by No 28 (AC) Squadron at RAF Benson and is the first of a new generation of advanced, medium support helicopters for the RAF. It is an all weather, day and night, multi-role helicopter used in both tactical and strategic operational roles. The aircraft carries an impressive defensive-aids suite, which includes a Radar and Laser Warning Receiver, Missile Approach Warners and Directional Infrared Countermeasures equipment, all integrated with an automatic chaff and flare dispensing system. This is one of the most comprehensive defensive-aids suites fitted to any helicopter in the world.

To ensure accurate navigation anywhere on the globe, the aircraft's management computers take data from its laser-gyro, inertial-navigation platform and its doppler system and from air data sources, and combine the information with precise position data received from Global Positioning System satellites.

Navigation at night is enhanced by the crew's use of night-vision goggles and by the aircraft's multi-function turret, which can be fitted with forward-looking infrared radar. To increase the aircraft's range, the Merlin is equipped with extended-range fuel tanks and is capable of air-to-air refuelling. Further range can be achieved by shutting down the third engine during the cruising phase of flight. It is also fitted with an active vibration-damping system, which reduces the level of noise and vibration inside the cabin to a level no greater than that of a turboprop aircraft. As a result, crew fatigue is much reduced during long transits and airframe life is increased.

The Merlin is able to carry a diverse range of bulky cargo, either internally or under-slung. Cargo can include artillery, Land Rovers or light-strike vehicles and over five tonnes of freight. The spacious cabin can also accommodate up to 24 fully equipped combat troops and, when required, will convert to carry 16 stretchers for casualty evacuation or during humanitarian and disaster relief operations. Designed to operate away from base workshops and in difficult terrain, the Merlin has state-of-the-art support technology and incorporates aircraft health-and-usage diagnostics and a self-test capability for ease of maintenance.

The Merlin is armed with two general purpose machine guns converted for the air role, although there is provision for additional weaponry to be fitted at a later date. ◼

Merlin HC3 port profile

Two Merlin HC3s transit cross-country at low level

Powerplant:

	Two Turbomeca Turmo
	3-C4 turbines
Thrust:	1300shp each
Length:	14.08m
Width:	3.00m
Height:	4.54m
Rotor span:	15.09m
Max T/O weight:	7400kg
Speed:	147kts
Ceiling:	17,000ft

The Puma HC1 first entered service in 1971, and the RAF currently has a fleet of 33 aircraft available to the front-line Support Helicopter Force. The aircraft are operated by No 33 Squadron, which is based at RAF Benson, and by No 230 Squadron, which is based at RAF Aldergrove, in Northern Ireland. No 33 Squadron, which is divided into two flights and the operational conversion flight, offers flexibility in its role in that the aircraft of one of the flights are fitted with desert warfare specialist equipment, while the aircraft of the other flight are fitted with arctic warfare specialist equipment.

The Pumas are used as battlefield helicopters within the Joint Helicopter Command and provide tactical troop and load movement by day or by night. The aircraft can carry 16 fully-equipped troops, or up to two tonnes of freight carried either internally or as an underslung load. The other major role is that of casualty or medical evacuation support, for which up to six stretchers can be fitted.

Each aircraft is equipped with satellite-based GPS equipment and an instrument landing system, enabling the aircraft to be navigated accurately and to be landed at suitably equipped airfields in poor weather conditions. The normal crew of two pilots, or a pilot and a weapons systems officer, plus a crewman, is trained in procedural instrument flying and tactical low flying by day and by night using night-vision goggles. The aircrew and their supporting ground crew are also trained to operate from inhospitable areas in all conditions ranging from desert to arctic environments.

For self-defence, the Puma is being upgraded with a new defensive-aids suite. This suite includes an integrated radar warning receiver, an AAR47 missile-approach-warning system, an ALQ 144 infrared jammer and automatic chaff and flare dispensing equipment. In addition, two cabin-mounted 7.62mm general purpose machine guns can be fitted for use by the crewmen. ∎

Puma HC1

Puma HC1 in the Arctic environment

RAF SIGNALS

In the context of the RAF, the term 'Signals' dates back to the RAF's formation during the First World War and encompassed all forms of communications. In today's high-technology, mobile and flexible force; the term is still retained in the title of a number of units whose responsibilities have now extended into computing, intelligence support and information exploitation.

Tactical Communications Wing
The largest RAF Signals Unit is the Tactical Communications Wing (TCW), which provides specialist teams of personnel at high readiness, equipped and trained to operate, protect and sustain the vital communications systems deployed on operations and exercises around the globe. With the world remaining an uncertain place, and with ever-greater emphasis placed upon expeditionary operations, TCW personnel, some 650 of them, are now required to deliver information and communications services (ICS) in a host of physically and electronically hostile environments. Since its origins in the 1960s, the TCW has supported a huge number of military operations by providing ICS to deployed squadrons, HQs and other Force Elements.

Today, the continually increasing reliance that operations have on modern digital communications and information technology means that TCW is bigger and busier than ever.

Information Services Support Unit
Another particularly significant Signals Unit is the Information Services Support Unit (ISSU),

TCW setting up a mobile comms station in Iraq

which provides crucial ICS in support of global operations, as well as support to the UK National and NATO elements based at HQ STC. Formed to develop ICS for the delivery of RAF Command and Control, the Unit is responsible for the management of the RAF's deployable Command, Control and Information System – the RAF's strategic IT system – which proved to be the key enabler of air command and control throughout Operation Telic in Iraq and Operation Herrick in Afghanistan. The breadth and scale of the ISSU's primary task has increased in line with the dramatic increase in demand for the capabilities it provides.

591 Signals Unit
Dating back to 1952, No. 591 Signals Unit (591 SU) ranks amongst the longest established independent units in the RAF. The Unit's original role was to conduct defensive monitoring of military communications and today the fundamental role of the Unit remains focused on delivering vital components of information assurance to operational commanders

in joint theatres of operations. 591 SU is a highly mobile force that provides a versatile, deployable package to the particular needs of operational commanders. The Unit deployed in both Gulf Wars and continues to operate routinely in Iraq, the Balkans and Afghanistan.

Joint Special Signals Units
The RAF provides both real estate and manpower to several Joint Special Signals Units (JSSUs) both in the UK and around the world. Involved in the collection of communications intelligence, these units are manned by members of the Army, Navy and Air Force.

Cyprus, Gibraltar and Falkland Islands Signals Units
In Cyprus, Gibraltar and the Falkland Islands, previously separate elements have been combined to form joint service Signals Units, which provide ICS support to the military formations at these locations. The RAF contributes significantly to the manpower employed in these distant locations.

A mobile TACAN beacon, used by aircraft for navigation in operational theatres

One of RAF Signals' greatest assets is mobility

Command, Control, Communications, Computers and Intelligence Support Squadrons

Whilst not strictly Signals Units, the RAF has recently re-organised its on-airfield information and communications service support, to form Command, Control, Communications, Computers and Intelligence Support Squadrons (C4I Spt Sqns). The development of computer networks and the increasing requirement for improved information exploitation has moved the emphasis of on-airfield support structures from the traditional engineering functions towards information management and this has necessitated re-organisa-tion and re-training of many personnel. The increasing dependence upon networked systems and IT tools and applications makes the C4I Spt Sqn an essential part of a station's mission support organisation.

90 SU at RAF Leeming

From April 2006, there will be a significant change in the organisation of RAF 'signals', with the creation of a focus for all RAF expeditionary ICS at RAF Leeming. RAF Leeming will be the future home of TCW, part of the ISSU and ERAS formed under the banner of 90 Signals Unit. These units will be integrated to provide a coherent ICS capability for deployed operations. ∎

Under the £2.5bn Skynet 5 Private Finance Initiative (PFI) contract signed in October 2003, the UK MoD is procuring satellite communications services from Paradigm Secure Communications until 2018. In February 2005, Paradigm Secure Communications achieved the key 'In Service Date' (ISD) milestone, for the Skynet 5 PFI programme. This is the first and most challenging milestone since Paradigm signed the contract and marks a significant change in the way that long haul communications services are delivered to the UK Armed Forces. It is a major contribution to the realisation of the MoD Global Communications Network (GCN) architecture.

This milestone required a major upgrade of UK Satellite Ground Station facilities and the introduction of new service management processes. The upgraded system, including new terminals and network control centre, can support a full range of modern communications services. ISD lays the foundation for future roll-out of remote terminals and further capability enhancements including the Paradigm Modem System (PMS).

The achievement of ISD represents a strong endorsement of the Skynet 5 PFI structure. All parties within the Skynet 5 'Enterprise' have worked together to achieve this key milestone, resulting in excellent working relationships and high levels of cooperation between MoD and industry teams. At the same time, Paradigm has been delivering services and exceeding performance targets during a very busy period of deployed operations using the Skynet 4 satellites. The Skynet 5 system will provide reliable secure voice and data communications for combined operations in peacekeeping and under battlefield conditions.

EADS Astrium is contracted by Paradigm Secure Communications to be prime contractor for the design and build of the entire system including two new generation Skynet 5 spacecraft. Skynet 5A and 5B will be launched in 2006 and 2007 and progressively take over from the current Skynet 4 satellites. The company is also responsible for upgrading the existing spacecraft control and operation facilities in the United Kingdom.

The technologically advanced, fully-hardened Skynet 5 satellites, based on the proven Eurostar 3000 platform, will carry advanced UHF and SHF communications payloads with 15 active channels and extensive channel-to-beam flexibility, as well as multiple antennae for global and regional beams. Located over the Atlantic and Indian oceans in geosynchronous orbit, Skynet 5A and 5B will provide coverage from South America to the Far East. The design and manufacture of the two Skynet 5 satellites is at an advanced stage with the Service Module for 5A already having been shipped from the UK to the company's facility in Toulouse. The Communications Module, once assembly and testing is completed at EADS Astrium's Portsmouth site, was shipped to Toulouse in the summer of 2005. After satellite assembly, spacecraft system and environmental testing will be conducted before shipment to the launch site.

The ground segment programme has also been progressing well. In parallel with the UK infrastructure upgrades delivered earlier this year, EADS Astrium has been upgrading the Royal Navy's SCOT antenna systems across the fleet. The Company has recently completed installation and trials of the first Skynet 5 baseband system on a Royal Navy ship. Operational service has commenced and the full roll out to ship platforms is now underway. Land forces will also benefit from network enabled and enhanced milsatcom capability with the provision of 44 new rugged medium and large land tactical terminals with deployable 2.4m and 4.6m antennae.

The groundbreaking Skynet 5 PFI programme will deliver the most advanced and flexible satellite communications service with an increase in power and flexibility. The service will enable instantaneous voice, video and data transmission between users deployed in a wide range of operational scenarios. Individual requests for services to meet specific operational requirements are handled by Paradigm which provides 24/7 365-day support backed by EADS Astrium's expertise. ■

Artist's impression of the Skynet 5 satellite communications platform

Air Warfare Centre

The Air Warfare Centre's Mission is: 'To provide Integrated Mission Support to defence-wide units for operations and training.'

Headquartered at RAF Waddington, the central activity of the Air Warfare Centre (and its 1,000+ personnel) is the integration of mission support with the aim of providing information and advice to the warfighter that is timely, accurate and, most importantly, usable. Crucial to the output of the Air Warfare Centre are the 5 Operational Evaluation Units (OEUs). The OEUs conduct test and evaluation focussing on the operational employment of new and existing equipment and techniques. The Combat Systems arm of this development is conducted by two lodger units based at RAF Coningsby: the Fast Jet and Weapons OEU, operating Tornado F3, GR4, and Harrier GR9; and, the Typhoon OEU (17(R) Squadron). In terms of Combat Support, the Joint Air Transport Evaluation Unit at RAF Brize Norton is involved with the development of aerial transport and

Counter-measures dispensed from a Hercules C-130

Mission preparation for Tactical Leadership Training

delivery techniques for all MoD air vehicles. While the Air Transport and Air-to-Air Refuelling OEU at RAF Lyneham concentrates its efforts on fixed-wing aircraft (including A400M). Rotary-wing evaluation is carried out under the auspices of the Air Warfare Centre by RWOETU, a Joint Helicopter Command element. The pivotal position of air command and control, intelligence, surveillance, and reconnaissance are reflected within the Air Warfare Centre by an OEU at Waddington with responsibility for the test and evaluation of all platforms, systems and equipment within this group. Though not yet an OEU, the Joint Combat Aircraft Team are engaged in the preparation for testing, evaluation and mission

support of this system in 2 locations in the US.

Within the Tactics and Training Wing, specialist operators from all facets of air power assist in the translation of a raw product into easily usable techniques and advice. An additional remit of the Wing is the promotion of tactical leadership expertise and excellence. They facilitate the Combined Qualified Weapons Instructor Course Operational Flying Phase and conduct Tactical Leadership Training of air elements. These courses culminate in large-force Combined Air Operations training events involving up to 50 or more aircraft from within STC, MoD, and abroad.

The AWC has responsibility for the provision of air intelligence to

A Typhoon F2 of 17(R) Sqn departs on a trials mission

Tornado from the inside out

Harrier GR9 of the FJWOEU

© Paul Bunch

MoD units. The Operational Support Centre has direct links with STC, PJHQ and operational theatres. Using the principle of 'reachback', commanders at all levels are able to link into the Centre direct from home-base or operational theatres.

Electronic Warfare Operational Support is provided in many forms and accessible through secure IT-based portals. Production of EW Mission Data for equipment is a central role of the unit and resting within the Air Warfare Centre is the Defence Electronic Warfare Centre with its attendant database. Though EW support is only a small paragraph within this handbook it is a key activity of the Air Warfare Centre with ramifications defence-wide.

The Air Warfare Centre also provides specialist input into the development of doctrine and command and control techniques – including conceptual development and experimentation. The Air Warfare Centre at Cranwell conducts Air Warfare Training courses ranging from the basic course for candidates undergoing initial training, through the Masters Degree level Aerosystems Course, to supporting Higher Command and Staff Courses with specialist presenters and has responsibility for the introduction of the RAF's Air Warfare Training Strategy.

The broad-range of experience and specialisation of its personnel, allied with its wide span of activity, enable the Air Warfare Centre to integrate and fuse information in order to meet its Mission of providing Integrated Mission Support to defence-wide units for operations and training. ◼

FLYING TRAINING

The Tucano T1 provides basic flying training from RAF Linton-on-Ouse

© Geoffrey Lee

Flying Training

Hawk T1A of 19(R) Squadron at RAF Valley
© Geoffrey Lee

The Royal Air Force enjoys a world-class reputation for the quality of its flying training, which has evolved over many decades into the current system. All RAF non-operational flying training is managed from the Training Group (TG) Headquarters at RAF Innsworth, near Gloucester. RAF ab-initio flying training is divided into 5 main areas: elementary training for all pilot streams, fast-jet pilot, multi-engine pilot, helicopter pilot and rearcrew. In addition, the Central Flying School (CFS) provides training for the qualified flying instructors, of all types, who staff the system. The Training Group also provides non-operational flying training for Royal Navy and Army pilots. All potential aircrew entrants to the RAF are first put through the 3-day aptitude and selection process at the Officer and Aircrew Selection Centre at RAF Cranwell. Following Initial Officer (or Non-Commissioned Officer) Training, trainee aircrew spend from 1-3 years in flying training at one or more of the TG airfields at Cranwell, Shawbury, Linton-on-Ouse and Valley. On completion of this, during which brevets are awarded, aircrew proceed to an Operational Conversion Unit (OCU) to continue their training on a specific type of operational aircraft. Large parts of the FT system are Joint-Service and most support aspects of the system are delivered by civilian contractors, including the provision of aircraft and instructors at the Defence Elementary Flying Training School (DEFTS) and the Defence Helicopter Flying School (DHFS).

Looking to the future, major developments are planned for the FT system to ensure it continues to meet the requirements of the front line of all 3 Services as the next generation of military aircraft come into service over the next decade and beyond, including: Typhoon F2, JCA, A400M, Sentinel, Nimrod MRA4, BRH, FRC, SCMR, Apache and Airbus A330 Tanker. The UK Military Flying Training System (UKMFTS) will replace the present FT arrangements from 2007. It is a Tri-Service programme that will cater for the different training needs of the entire flying element of the UK front line. More details of the UKMFTS are contained in the Future Equipment section. ■

Advanced Flying Training: Hawk T1/1A

Powerplant:
Rolls-Royce Turbomeca
Adour turbofan
Thrust: 5200lbs
Wing span: 9.39m
Length: 11.9m
Height: 3.99m
Max T/O weight: 5700kg
Speed: 550kts
Ceiling: 48,000ft

Weapons:
AIM-9L Sidewinder
Aden 30mm cannon
BL755 cluster bomb

The Hawk first entered service with the RAF in 1976, both as an advanced flying-training aircraft and a weapons-training aircraft. The Hawk T1 version is currently used at RAF Valley for fast-jet pilot advanced flying training with No 208(R) Squadron, and at RAF Scampton by the RAF Aerobatic Team, the Red Arrows. The T1A is used for weapons and tactical training on No 19(R) Squadron at RAF Valley, and by No 100 Squadron at RAF Leeming for advanced fast-jet weapons systems officer training and operational support-flying. In its weapons and tactical training role the Hawk is used to teach air combat, air-to-air firing, air-to-ground firing and low-flying techniques and operational procedures.

The Hawk is an all-metal, low-wing, tandem seat aircraft of conventional design. The wing has a moderate sweep with 2° dihedral and trailing edge slotted flaps. A one-piece all-moving tailplane is also swept back with 10° dihedral. The fuselage comprises three main parts. The front fuselage accommodates two equipment bays and a pressurised cabin containing two tandem cockpits. The centre fuselage contains the engine, a fuselage fuel tank, a gas turbine starting system and a ram air turbine; the latter providing emergency hydraulic power should the two normal hydraulic systems fail. The rear fuselage houses the jet pipe bay and an airbrake hinged to its under surface.

The Hawk is powered by a Rolls-Royce Turbomeca Adour 151 turbofan engine, which is an un-reheated version of the engine powering the Jaguar GR3 aircraft.

While the Hawk T1 is used solely in the advanced flying-training role, the Hawk T1A is equipped to an operational standard and is capable of undertaking a number of war roles. The T1A has two under-wing pylons cleared to carry BL755 cluster bombs or Sidewinder AIM-9L air-to-air missiles, and can carry a 30mm Aden cannon in a pod underneath the fuselage centre-line. The cannon can be fired at the same time as any of the pylon-mounted weapons are selected for release or firing. Aiming facilities for the aircraft's attack modes are provided by an integrated strike and interception system, while a Vinten video recording system is used to record the weapon sighting.

The next generation Hawk aircraft, the Hawk 128, will enter service in 2008 as a replacement for some of the current Hawk TMk1s. The Hawk 128 will introduce student pilots to the digital cockpit environment they will experience in front-line operational service and will provide a seamless transition between basic flying training, and operational conversion training onto advanced fighter aircraft such as the Typhoon F2 and the Joint Combat Aircraft. ■

Hawk T1A port profile

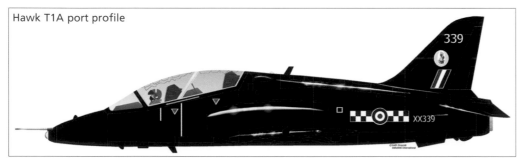

Hawk T1As from RAF Valley

© *Geoffrey Lee*

Powerplant:
Two Rolls-Royce Viper Mk 301 turbojets	
Thrust:	3310lbs each
Wing span:	14.33m
Length:	14.48m
Height:	4.87m
Max T/O weight:	21,000lbs
Speed:	284kts
Ceiling:	42,000ft

The Dominie T1, which has been in RAF service since 1965, is the military training version of the Hawker Siddeley 125 twin-jet business aircraft. A total of nine aircraft are operated by No 55(R) Squadron at the RAF College Cranwell, where they are used to train weapon systems officers and operators, air engineers and air loadmasters in systems management, air leadership, decision making and teamwork to meet the operational demands of the RAF.

In 1996 the aircraft underwent a major upgrade programme, with the installation of a modern avionics suite and a new systems installation and cabin layout, completed under contract by Racal and Marshall Aerospace. The design features included installation of a Super Searcher Ground-mapping Radar, which was fully integrated with the aircraft's associated radio equipment, avionics systems, multicolour displays and navigation mission-computer.

The Dominie T1 has a maximum crew of six and is generally operated with one pilot captain, with the remaining aircrew comprising a balance of up to five students and instructors. Training sorties are usually of two to three hours' duration and are flown in a mixture of regimes dependent on the stage of training and the exercise requirements. These sorties include a mix of low-level flying, maritime operations, radar handling and targeting training. Medium level, high level and general-handling sorties are flown for other training requirements, including trials flights conducted for the Air Warfare Centre at RAF Waddington. ■

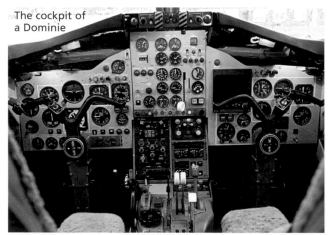
The cockpit of a Dominie

Dominie T1 on the flight line at RAF College Cranwell

A Dominie takes to the skies

Powerplant:

Two Pratt & Whitney PT6A-42 Turboprops	
Rating:	850 shp each
Wingspan:	16.61m
Length:	13.36m
Height:	4.52m
Max T/O weight:	5670kg
Speed:	259kts
Ceiling:	28,000ft

The Beech King Air B200, the newest training aircraft in the RAF inventory, is a twin-engine turboprop monoplane, which first entered RAF service in 2004. It is used as an advanced, multi-engine pilot trainer by No 45(R) Squadron, which is part of No 3 Flying Training School based at RAF Cranwell, in Lincolnshire. Prior to flying the King Air, students who have been streamed to fly multi-engine aircraft at the end of elementary flying training undertake survival training and personal development training to prepare them for the rigours of operational service. They then join No 45(R) Squadron, and receive an additional 30 hours training on the multi-engine lead-in (MELIN) course, flying Firefly 260 aircraft. During the MELIN course, students are taught crew co-operation and procedural flying skills to prepare them for their advanced flying training on the King Air.

The King Air course is split into basic and advanced phases. In the basic phase, students learn essential multi-engine techniques such as general handling, asymmetric flying, emergency handling and radio-aids navigation, and consolidate the multi-crew skills acquired on the MELIN. In the advanced phase, the emphasis shifts towards developing captaincy, crew resource management, and managing the King Air's advanced avionics systems. Students learn advanced skills such as formation flying, low-level flying and airways navigation, and are expected to plan and manage composite missions involving several aircraft.

On completion of the course students are awarded their coveted pilot's wings, and then undertake conversion to their frontline aircraft type at an Operational Conversion Unit.

A variety of courses are available using the King Air, based mainly on the student's previous flying experience. This experience can be as little as 100 hours for a student arriving straight from elementary flying training, to a few thousand hours for a qualified pilot transferring to the multi-engine role. In addition to its flying training role, the King Air can be used to carry up to 6 passengers or freight.

The King Air B200 has performed extremely well in its first year of service, and has proved popular with students and instructors alike. Its combination of a well-proven airframe with advanced cockpit and systems make it an ideal training platform for the new generation of multi-engine aircraft entering RAF service. ■

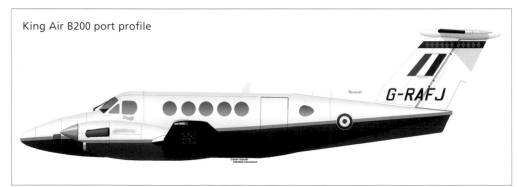

King Air B200 port profile

Two King Airs at medium altitude

Powerplant:

Textron Lycoming flat six-cylinder engine

Rating:	260hp
Wingspan:	10.72m
Length:	7.48m
Height:	2.29m
Max T/O weight:	1159kg
Max range:	650nmls
Speed:	154kts
Ceiling:	10,000ft

The Firefly T67 M260, which entered RAF service in 1996, is a two-seat aircraft used at the RAF College Cranwell for training pilots who have completed elementary flying training and have been selected for multi-engine training on the King Air B200. The aircraft are civilian registered and are owned, supplied and maintained by Babcock Defence Services, who provide the aircraft under contract to the RAF. The Firefly is used on a Multi-Engine Lead-In (MELIN) course, which is an integral part of the role of the King Air training squadron, No 45 (R) Squadron. The course gives student pilots an insight into more advanced flying than they encounter on the elementary course and comprises general handling, procedural instrument flying, low-level navigation, formation flying, night flying and an introduction to dual-crew operations.

The Firefly, made in glass fibre by Slingsby Aviation in Yorkshire, is a single piston-engined aircraft with a 260hp Textron-Lycoming engine, which drives a three-blade, constant-speed, composite propeller. Its instrumentation and communications equipment allows it to be flown along airways and the aircraft is cleared for instrument flying and night flying. The Firefly is fitted with side-by-side dual controls, a fixed windscreen and a backward-tilting canopy incorporating direct ventilation windows and fresh-air scoops. The unpressurised aircraft is fully aerobatic and can easily maintain height during an aerobatic sequence. The aircraft also has fuel and oil systems capable of sustaining inverted flight.

The Firefly can carry two pilots for over three hours of training. This endurance, coupled with a rapid climb rate of less than 10 minutes to reach 10,000ft, make it an excellent training aircraft. ∎

Firefly cockpit

The Firefly is fully aerobatic

Powerplant:
Ariel 1D1 gas-turbine
engine
Thrust: 625shp
Length: 12.94m
Fuselage length: 10.93m
Height: 3.2m
Rotor diameter: 10.69m
Max T/O weight: 2100kg
Speed: 155kts
Ceiling: 16,000ft

The Squirrel HT1 is used by the Defence Helicopter Flying School (DHFS) at RAF Shawbury, in Shropshire, for Single Engine Basic Rotary Wing (SEBRW) training with No 660 Squadron and Single Engine Advanced Rotary Wing (SEARW) training with No 705 Squadron. The DHFS selected the Squirrel helicopter, manufactured by Eurocopter, as a replacement for the Gazelle when the School became operational in 1997, and since that date the 26 aircraft in service have amassed over 100,000 hours flying time between them. Powered by a single Ariel 1D1 gas-turbine engine, which drives a conventional three-blade main rotor and a twin-blade tail rotor, the Squirrel is an ideal platform to teach the rudiments of rotary-wing flying. It has an endurance of three hours, a cruising speed of 115 kts (132mph) and seating for a crew of two and four passengers. The Squirrel can be configured either to meet the demands of SEBRW and SEARW, or to meet any secondary transport or communication tasks.

The initial flying-training course with No 660 Squadron, the Army Air Corps (AAC) element of DHFS, teaches basic rotary-wing skills and emergency handling, culminating in a first solo and a handling check prior to SEARW training. The SEARW phase of the course, run by 705 Squadron, the Fleet Air Arm element of DHFS, is where basic skills are consolidated and developed into more applied techniques. The syllabus includes non-procedural instrument flying, basic night flying, low-level and formation flying, mountain flying and an introduction to winching for RN students. In addition to DHFS, the Squirrel HT1 is used by the Central Flying School (Helicopter) Squadron at RAF Shawbury for instructor training, and by 670 AAC Squadron, based at Middle Wallop, in Hampshire, for operational training. ∎

Single engined Squirrel port profile

Squirrel is used to teach advanced single-engine rotary-wing flight skills

Powerplant:

Two Pratt & Whitney PT6T-3D turboshafts

Thrust:	1800shp combined
Length:	17.11m
Fuselage length:	12.7m
Height:	3.48m
Rotor diameter:	14.02m
Max T/O weight:	5409kg
Speed:	140kts
Ceiling:	20,000ft

The Griffin HT1 is used as an advanced flying-training helicopter at the Defence Helicopter Flying School (DHFS) at RAF Shawbury, in Shropshire, and the Search and Rescue Training Unit (SARTU) at RAF Valley, in Anglesey. There are eleven aircraft in service; eight are based at RAF Shawbury and three are based at RAF Valley. The Griffin HT1 is a military twin-engined helicopter derived from the civilian Bell Textron 412EP helicopter and is powered by two Pratt & Whitney turboshafts rated at 1800shp. The aircraft has an advanced, composite material, four-blade main rotor system, and pendulum dampers on the rotor hub to reduce vibrations at higher cruise speeds. The composite main-blades can be interchanged and folded easily for storage.

With a cruising speed of 120kts (138mph) and an endurance of 2¾ hours, the Griffin HT1 is ideally suited for Multi-engine Advanced Rotary Wing (MEARW) training, which is completed over a period of 34 weeks on No 60(R) Squadron at RAF Shawbury. The syllabus includes general-handling flying, underslung-load carrying, night-vision goggle training, procedural instrument flying, forma-

Griffin HT1 practising rough-ground landing techniques

tion flying, low-flying navigation and an introduction to tactical employment, including operations from confined areas. A short SAR-procedures course, which includes elements of mountain flying and maritime rescue winching, is conducted at RAF Valley. However, students who are finally streamed for SAR flying duties on completion of their advanced helicopter training return to SARTU to complete an extended SAR course prior to joining the Sea King Operational Conversion Unit at RAF St Mawgan.

In addition to pilot training, the Griffin is used for crewman training: a very important and integral part of multi-crew operations. A Griffin simulator, with full motion capability and an advanced graphics suite, is also based at RAF Shawbury and is a fully integrated part of the MEARW course. It is especially useful for procedural instrument-flying training and practising complex emergency-handling techniques. The Griffin, which has now been in service with DHFS for five years, is also used in its HAR2 form by No 84 Squadron on SAR duties in Cyprus. ◼

Helicopter aircrew must be competent over all terrains and operating environments

Basic Flying Training: Tucano T1

Powerplant:

	Garrett TPE331-12B
	turboprop
Thrust:	1150shp
Wing span:	11.28m
Length:	9.86m
Height:	3.4m
Max T/O weight:	3182kg
Speed:	300kts
Ceiling:	30,000ft

The Tucano T1 is a modified version of the Brazilian Embraer EMB-312 Tucano aircraft, and is built under licence by Shorts of Belfast. The Tucano is operated primarily from No 1 Flying Training School, at RAF Linton-on-Ouse, to provide basic fast-jet flying training to RAF and RN student pilots, and basic WSO training to all potential RAF WSOs. Student pilots fly around 130 hours during their training course on the Tucano before progressing to the Hawk T1 aircraft at RAF Valley.

The aircraft is powered by an 1150shp Garrett Turboprop engine, has a maximum speed of 300kts (345mph) and can maintain 270kts (310mph) at low level. It can operate at up to 30,000 feet and has an initial climb rate of 4000 feet per minute. The Tucano replaced the Jet Provost in RAF service and its two-seat tandem cockpit makes it an ideal lead-in to the Hawk, which is flown at the next stage of training. The turboprop Tucano was chosen to replace the RAF's Jet Provosts because of its greater fuel efficiency and lower operating costs.

The aircraft handling is similar to that of a jet aircraft and it is fully aerobatic, thus providing an excellent workhorse for training fast-jet pilots in all aspects of military flying. It is used to develop students in a full range of skills, including general aircraft handling, formation flying and low-level navigation and, due to its comprehensive avionics and ice-protection packages, it can be flown in all types of weather, by day and by night. The Tucano's all-weather flying capability, plus its excellent endurance, allows a great measure of flexibility in the training role. Should weather conditions be poor at their home base, crews operating from RAF Linton-on-Ouse can fly low-level sorties to locations as far away as Wales or the north of Scotland.

The Tucano has recently undergone a wing and fuselage strengthening programme to overcome aircraft stress problems and will remain as the RAF's primary fast-jet basic flying-training aircraft until later in the decade. ∎

Tucano T1 port profile

The Tucano is designed to provide a seamless transition onto fast-jet training

Elementary Flying Training: Tutor

Powerplant:
Textron Lycoming AE-360-B
piston engine
Rating: 180hp
Wingspan: 10.00m
Length: 7.79m
Height: 2.82m
Max T/O weight: 992kg
Speed: 135kts
Ceiling: 10,000ft

The Grob 115E, known by the RAF as the Tutor, is used for Elementary Flying Training by the 14 University Air Squadrons and 12 Air Experience Flights throughout the UK. It is also used by the Central Flying School and for elementary WSO training at the RAF College Cranwell. All of the Tutors in RAF service are entered on the UK Civil Aircraft Register and are provided by Vosper Thornycroft Aviation.

Tutor port profile

The Tutor is constructed mainly from carbonfibre reinforced plastic, which combines high strength with light weight. Like its predecessor, the Bulldog, the Tutor has side-by-side seating but, unlike the Bulldog, the primary flight instruments are on the right-hand side of the cockpit. This allows the student to fly the aircraft from the right-hand seat with a right-hand stick and a left-hand throttle so that future transition to fast-jet aircraft is made easier.

Unpressurised, and powered by a Textron-Lycoming 180hp piston engine driving a Hoffman three-bladed, constant-speed propeller, the Tutor can cruise at 130kts at sea level and climb to 5,000ft in seven minutes. The aircraft has a very clean airframe and has a three-minute invert-ed-flight time limit, making it ideal for aerobatics where, unlike previous RAF light aircraft, it loses little or no height during a full aerobatic sequence. The aircraft has a very modern instrument and avionics suite, including a Differential Global Positioning System, which, apart from giving excellent navigational information, can also be used to generate a simulated Instrument Landing System (ILS) approach for training use at airfields where ILS ground equipment is not fitted for the runway in use.

The Tutor is a cost-effective, modern elementary training aircraft. The combination of docile handling characteristics and good performance make it very suitable for its training role. ∎

The Tutor's instrumentation is easy to read

A Tutor makes its way through a cloud bank at medium altitude

Powerplant:
Grob 2500E1 horizontally opposed four-cylinder, air-cooled engine
Rating:	95hp
Length:	8.10m
Height:	1.70m
Wingspan:	17.40m
Max T/O weight:	908kg
Speed:	130kts
Ceiling:	8,000ft

The Grob 109B motor glider, known by the RAF as the Vigilant T1, is used by the Air Cadet Organisation to give basic flying and gliding training to air cadets. The aircraft is built in Germany, but it has been modified to meet the RAF's training requirements by the inclusion of an additional throttle in the cockpit and an increase in the maximum take-off weight. The Vigilant is currently used by 16 Volunteer Gliding Squadrons (VGSs), located at various sites around the UK. Their role is to train air cadets in basic flying techniques and to enable them to reach a standard where they are able to fly solo. Courses available to the air cadets are the gliding induction course, the gliding scholarship course and the advanced gliding

The Vigilant's undercarriage is non-retractable. Note the wide tailplane.

training course. The Vigilant T1 aircraft is also used at the Air Cadet Central Gliding School, at Syerston, in Nottinghamshire, where it is used to train the VGS instructors.

The aircraft is powered by a Grob 2500E1 horizontally opposed, four-cylinder, air-cooled engine, which provides a direct drive to a Hoffman Ho-V62 R/L160BT variable-pitch, two-bladed propeller. The conventional landing gear, which is non-retractable, comprises two main wheels with fairings, and a tailwheel, which is steered through the rudder pedals. A retrofitted throttle is provided for use by the left-hand seat, giving the student the familiar military configuration of right-hand stick and left-hand throttle arrangement.

The Vigilant TMk1 is a cost-effective, modern aircraft. Its docile handling characteristics, combined with good fuel economy, make it an excellent training aircraft for cadets and instructors alike. ■

Vigilant port profile

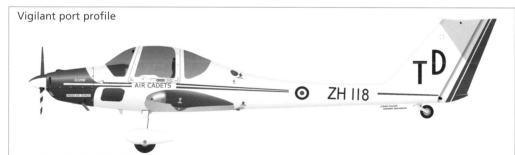

The Grob G103A Twin II Acro, known by the RAF as the Viking T1, is used by the Air Cadet Organisation to give basic gliding training to air cadets. The aircraft is currently used by 11 Volunteer Gliding Squadrons located at various sites around the UK. Their role is to train air cadets to a standard that will allow them to fly solo. Courses available to the air cadets are the gliding induction course, the gliding scholarship course and the advanced gliding training course. The aircraft is again also used at the Air Cadet Central Gliding School, at Syerston, where it is used in the training of the VGS instructors.

The Viking T1 is a high performance sailplane, which can be winch-launched or aero-towed. The aircraft is fitted with a non-retractable tandem undercarriage and upper surface air-brakes. It has tandem seating for a crew of two and is constructed using the latest techniques in industrial glass-reinforced plastic for light weight and strength. The Viking is used for basic training, high-performance flying and simple aerobatic flying and is a cost-effective, modern glider, ideally suited to its training role with the Air Cadet Organisation. ■

A Viking T1 soaring at high level

A Viking swoops over the English countryside with an Air Cadet at the controls

Powerplant:
The aircraft can be winch launched or aero-towed

Length:	8.18m
Height:	1.55m
Wingspan:	17.50m
Max T/O weight:	625kg
Speed:	135kts
Ceiling:	8,000ft

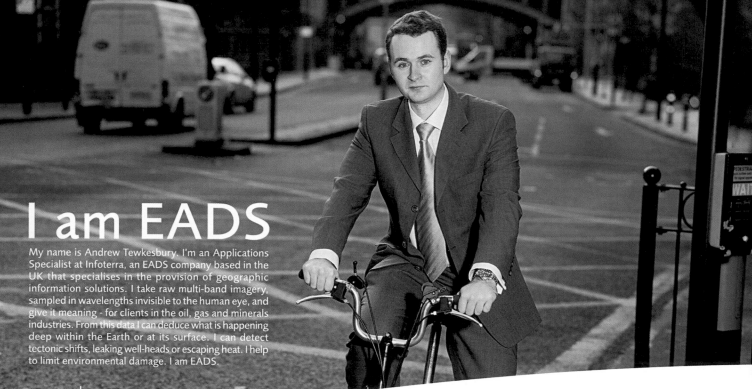

I am EADS

My name is Andrew Tewkesbury. I'm an Applications Specialist at Infoterra, an EADS company based in the UK that specialises in the provision of geographic information solutions. I take raw multi-band imagery, sampled in wavelengths invisible to the human eye, and give it meaning - for clients in the oil, gas and minerals industries. From this data I can deduce what is happening deep within the Earth or at its surface. I can detect tectonic shifts, leaking well-heads or escaping heat. I help to limit environmental damage. I am EADS.

www.eads.com

AIRBUS   EUROCOPTER   EUROFIGHTER   A400M   METEOR   GALILEO   ARIANE

EADS

The step beyond

University Air Squadrons

Air Experience Flying

There are 14 flying Univerity Air Squadrons (UASs) spread throughout the UK, each linked to several universities and an airfield. Their main aim is to show young men and women undergraduates what life is like in the RAF, interest them in flying and possibly a career in the RAF. The UAS system is responsible for delivering 60% of the RAF's pilot intake each year, all of whom will have completed the elementary flying training course while at university. Although most UAS members are interested in flying with the RAF, there has been a great increase in the number of students wishing to enter the Ground Branches of the service; therefore a formal Ground Branch syllabus has been introduced, which includes an Air Experience Course. A major review of UAS training has recently taken place and under the new system aircrew training will take place after the student has graduated, rather being spread throughout his time at university. UAS students will be offered personal development and leadership training while at university, followed by flying training once they have graduated. ■

As part of their air experience flying, Air Cadets have the opportunity to fly with RAF pilots in Grob Tutor aircraft at one of 12 Air Experience Flights (AEFs) situated at various airfields around the UK. AEF aircraft are flown by volunteer pilots, all of whom are current or former Service pilots. The cadets receive ground instruction on the principles of flight, how to prepare the aircraft for flight and how to carry out minor maintenance tasks. They then get airborne, where they are given the chance to control the aeroplane, experience aerobatics or simply admire the view from the air. The AEF task is based on a minimum of 20 minutes flying per cadet per year and all Air Cadets get the opportunity to fly with the AEF each year. Many Air Cadets also get the opportunity to fly in a variety of other RAF aircraft, including, for some lucky individuals, passenger flights in fast jets. During their 'careers', many Air Cadets will have flown in a variety of Service aeroplanes and helicopters. Those Air Cadets with an aptitude for flying can apply for a number of courses, including Flying and Gliding Scholarships. ■

A student pilot conducts a pre-flight inspection of a Tutor on the flight-line

AEF flying – an experience not to be missed

The Fast Jet & Weapons Operational Evaluation Unit (FJWOEU) was officially formed at RAF Coningsby on 1 April 2004. It is the amalgamation of the Strike/Attack OEU, originally from RAF Boscombe Down, the Air Guided Weapons OEU from RAF Valley, and the Tornado F3 OEU, which was already based at RAF Coningsby.

The Unit has three main areas of activity and responsibility: it conducts operational testing and evaluation of aircraft and any related equipment; supports the development of future equipment, software and aircraft related concepts; and provides accurate and timely advice to enhance aircraft survivability against air-to-air and surface-to-air threats. The Unit spends most of its time working on new systems and technology or upgrades to existing software and works closely with experts at QinetiQ and BAE Systems. It is useful for manufacturers to have early feedback from the people who will actually be operating their systems, so there are occasions when the Unit will be involved with a new aircraft or system from the outset. The most common misconception about the FJWOEU is that its function is to test aircraft. In fact, the Unit is not responsible for the testing of actual aircraft – they have already been proven airworthy and are in service – their principal concern is testing of the new systems or procedures that have been developed, or are being developed, for the aircraft.

The FJWOEU undertakes a number of projects each month that are conducted in order of priority. Some projects will be carried out when the system or upgrade is introduced, others may be archived for later attention, whilst a few will be top secret, cutting edge and urgent. If, for example, an adversary develops a new missile, appropriate experts would quickly develop countermeasures and evasion tactics. These would then be applied to the aircraft and tested by the FJWOEU, before being sent out to the frontline with accompanying detailed instructions, operating guidelines and limits.

Commanded by a RAF Wing Commander fast-jet pilot, there are around 170 people within the FJWOEU – aircrew (pilots and weapon systems officers), engineers, weapons experts, administration staff, as well as an advisory test pilot and a civilian scientist who is in charge of the analysis team. Their stable of aircraft comprises three Tornado F3s, three Tornado GR4s, one Jaguar GR3, three Harrier GR9s and a Harrier GR7, all of which are based at RAF Coningsby and are entirely at the Unit's disposal. The FJWOEU works on all RAF fast-jet types, with the exception of the Hawk, which is not used operationally by the RAF, and the Typhoon. As the Typhoon is new to service, there are too many projects associated with this aircraft alone for it to fall under the wing of the FJWOEU. The Typhoon OEU is, however, located just down the corridor from the FJWOEU team, allowing frequent, vital liaison between the Weapons team and the Typhoon OEU as the first crucial live weapon-firing trials begin for the RAF's latest fast jet. ■

Jaguar GR3 and Tornado F3 at low level

© Paul Bunch

Harrier GR9 conducting high-speed high-manoeuvrability trials

© Paul Bunch

RED ARROWS AEROBATIC DISPLAY TEAM

Acknowledged as one of the world's premier aerobatic teams, the RAF Aerobatic Team, the Red Arrows, is the public face of the Royal Air Force. The Red Arrows promote the professional excellence of the RAF, assist in recruiting into the RAF, contribute to Defence Diplomacy, and support wider British interests through the promotion of British industry overseas.

The Red Arrows consists of over 100 officers and airmen and airwomen drawn from all trades and disciplines throughout the RAF. Officially formed on 1 March 1965, the Team has now performed over 3800 displays in 52 different countries. The Team's home base is RAF Scampton, in Lincolnshire.

All nine Red Arrows display pilots are fast-jet pilots from front-line RAF squadrons. In 2005, the Team has pilots from all four front-line fast-jet types; Jaguar GR3, Tornado GR4, Tornado F3 and Harrier GR7. To apply for selection to The Red Arrows, pilots must have amassed a minimum of 1500 flying hours, have completed one front-line tour and be assessed as

Classic Reds crowd-front break

above average in their particular flying role. Competition for selection is extremely stiff; each year between 35 and 40 pilots apply for the three vacant positions on the Team. On completion of their three-year tour with The Red Arrows, the pilots either return to front line operational squadrons or to instructional or staff duties.

Reds 1 to 5 form the front section known as 'Enid', and Reds 6 to 9 are known as 'Gypo'. The Synchro Pair, Reds 6 and 7, perform the highly popular, dynamic manoeuvres during the second half of the display sequence. There is one other qualified Hawk pilot: Red 10, who flies a tenth Hawk to

display venues ready for use in case one of the other nine aircraft becomes unserviceable. Red 10's two primary roles on the ground at every display are to act as the Team's Safety Officer, maintaining two-way radio contact with the Team Leader throughout the display, and as the Team Commentator.

Efficient planning and organisation are vital if 10 aircraft, together with their support staff and equipment are to arrive safely and fully prepared at a display venue. Keeping The Red Arrows in the air is a complex, time-consuming process. Apart from the pilots, there are two Engineering

Officers, a Team Manager, an Adjutant, a Public Relations Officer (the only civilian on the Team), and approximately 85 ground technicians and administrative staff. The support staff are known collectively as 'The Blues' and together they represent a broad cross-section of RAF technical and non-technical trades. Before each display, the Team Manager and Adjutant will have provided the event organiser with a document showing timings, transit routes, personnel involved and equipment required. The Junior Engineering Officer and nine engineering technicians, known as the 'Circus', fly in the rear seats of the Hawk aircraft to display locations to ensure any essential servicing can begin before the main support team arrives.

Typically, more than 300 requests for Red Arrows' displays are received annually, but only about 100 can ever be fitted into the programme. To try and meet as many requests as possible, the Team complete low-level flypasts at a large number of separate venues as they transit from display to display. ■

Reforming after a high-speed manoeuvre

© EJ.v.Koningsveld

In the years immediately following the Second World War, it became traditional for a Spitfire and Hurricane to lead the Victory Day flypast over London. From that event an idea grew to form an historic collection of flyable aircraft to commemorate the Battle of Britain and other major battles. Thus, in 1957, the Historic Aircraft Flight was formed at RAF Biggin Hill in what, even then, had become a predominantly jet-powered Air Force. For some years the Flight experienced variable fortune before emerging in its current form as one of the world's best-known historic collections fielding a Lancaster, a Dakota, five Spitfires, two Hurricanes and two Chipmunks.

The BBMF Lancaster is one of only two airworthy Lancasters left in the world from the 7,377 that were built during the war. Its unique shape and the marvellous sound of its four Rolls-Royce Merlin engines commemorate the courage and sacrifice of the aircrews of Bomber Command who lost their lives during the bombing campaigns of the war. The C47 Dakota is symbolic of the sacrifices of RAF Transport Command and also the men of the Parachute Regiment who parachuted from Dakotas in support of operations such as the D-Day invasion and Operation 'Market Garden' at Arnhem (the 'Bridge Too Far'). The Flight's five Spitfires and two Hurricanes commemorate the bravery and the vital contribution of the RAF fighter pilots. Spitfire MkIIA P7350 is the oldest airworthy Spitfire in the world and the only Spitfire to have actually flown in the Battle of Britain; it still has repaired bullet holes visible in its port wing, 'wounds' sustained in combat with German Bf 109s dur-

A Spitfire MkV and a Hurricane IIc of the BBMF executing a formation break

The classic trio of the Second World
War RAF in transit in vic formation

BBMF trio returning from a display

The Royal Air Force Handbook

ing October 1940. One of the BBMF Hurricanes (MkIIC PZ865) is the last Hurricane ever built out of a total of 14,533 ('The Last of the Many'); the Hurricanes represent the massive contribution that the aircraft made to victory during the Second World War, not least during the Battle of Britain, serving operationally every day throughout hostilities, in every operational theatre and in many different roles.

Since its inception in 1957, the aircrew on the Flight have been drawn from volunteers, all of whom perform a primary duty on front-line aircraft such as Typhoon, Tornado F3, Harrier GR7/9, Canberra PR9 and Boeing E-3D AWACs, or on training aircraft such as the Dominie and Super King Air. The one exception is the Officer Commanding for whom the demands of overseeing operations, administration and engineering dictate that he serves full time with the BBMF. In the early years, engineers, like the aircrew, were volunteers, but with the expansion of the fleet in the mid-1970s engineering was placed on a more formal basis and the team now consists of 25 full-time ground crew personnel led by a Warrant Officer Engineering Officer. These personnel handle all aspects of the maintenance of the BBMF's fleet of 11 historic aircraft, both at Coningsby and on the display circuit, with the exception of major (deep-strip) servicing, which is usually contracted out to Industry.

For many years after its formation in 1957, the Flight conducted relatively low-key operations, typically making 50-60 appearances per season, a situation that continued into the mid-1960s. By 1992 participation was up to 150 appearances, growing to 200 in 1995 and exceeding 500 in 1996. Since 2002 the Flight has successfully achieved well over 600 individual aircraft appearances during each year's display season and this is now considered the norm. The Flight's aircraft will appear at around 120 displays and 300 other events each year with an estimated audience of over 6 million people at the venues, plus many more who see the aircraft en route or at land-away airfields.

Spitfire MkV up close and personal

FUTURE EQUIPMENT

MoD Abbey Wood, Bristol, home
to DPA and DLO project teams

FUTURE EQUIPMENT

Procurement of new fighting equipment and supporting services for all three UK Armed Forces, and some overseas armed services, is undertaken by the MoD's Bristol-based Defence Procurement Agency (DPA).

The agency has an annual spend of about £6bn and was formed in 1999 from the then Procurement Executive as part of a series of major reforms of the way the MoD bought and supported equipment.

The DPA has about 60 integrated project teams, backed by some 20 specialist support groups. The agency manages several hundred projects at any one time with a total value of some £75bn and employs around 4,500 people, a mix of civilians and military personnel.

Projects range across all capability areas, from the Typhoon combat aircraft to research into the latest airborne targeting pod technologies. Some take a few months to complete, while others span more than a decade.

The agency also supports fielded forces by meeting Urgent Operational Requirements (UORs). The DPA delivered around 190 UORs worth in the region of £500 million in support of operations in Iraq in 2003.

As part of the reform of procurement the Defence Logistics Organisation was formed in 2000 to manage and improve all military support activities for the UK Armed Forces. It has its headquarters in Bath.

It too contains a range of about 60 integrated project teams covering the support and

MoD Main Building, the department's headquarters in Whitehall, central London

upgrade of equipment operated by the Armed Forces. Its annual budget is of the order of £8 bn and it employs around 20,000 people at more than 80 locations across the UK and around the world.

DLO staff, as in the DPA, are a mixture of civilian and military personnel.

Personnel from the DLO were, in 2005, supporting British Forces deployed on operations in Iraq, Afghanistan and the Balkans.

The DLO and DPA are working to harmonise their processes to ensure that efficiency is maximised. Integrated project teams hosted by the two organisations are accountable to both the Chief of Defence Procurement and the Chief of Defence Logistics and carry out work for either organisation. This gives a stronger focus to the

management of equipment throughout its life with the MoD.

Both organisations are undergoing further change to increase efficiency. In the DPA this involves the investment of more resources and intellectual effort in the early stages of projects in order to set more realistic performance, time and cost parameters that will provide a better basis for the major investment decision.

In the DLO the defence logistics transformation programme aims to improve effectiveness, reduce costs and improve flexibility in the support of operations.

Activities include simplifying support, partnering with industry and making the supply chain more responsive to the needs of commanders in the field. ■

Air-to-air BVR missile

Length:	3.67m
Speed:	Mach 4+
Guidance system:	Inertial mid-course/Active radar terminal
AIRCRAFT:	Typhoon F2

The Meteor missile is being procured under a £1.2 billion contract placed at the end of 2002 to meet the MoD's requirement for a Beyond-Visual-Range Air-to-Air Missile. It is expected to enter service on RAF Typhoon aircraft early next decade.

The weapon is being procured by an international industrial consortium led by MBDA and including companies in Germany, France, Italy, Sweden and Spain. The weapon is also expected to equip the French Rafale and Swedish Gripen fighter aircraft.

The programme had its genesis under Staff Requirement (A)1239 in the mid 1990s, which followed MoD studies that showed some highly agile future fighter designs could outrun or evade current air-to-air missiles at extreme range.

A range of studies ran into the late 1990s, when MoD received final bids from industry covering Meteor and a US candidate weapon. MoD selected Meteor as the winning contender in 2000.

Conventional rocket powered missiles use a boost motor to bring them to high supersonic speed, after which they glide to the target, losing energy when manoeuvring to close to within lethal range of their warheads.

Meteor is designed around an air-breathing ramjet which boosts the weapon away from the launch aircraft and then remains under power until warhead detonation, giving the missile the energy to pursue and destroy the fastest and most agile aircraft at range.

Fighters equipped with Meteor will be able to engage multiple targets simultaneously, at greater range than provided by existing weapons, in all weathers, day or night.

A stealthy launch technique will mean hostile aircraft receive the minimum warning that they are under attack and will have less opportunity to take evasive action.

Meteor will use the most advanced processors, combined with its own inertial navigation system, to head towards the target after launch. It can receive updates on target position from its launch aircraft – or other suitably equipped aircraft – when in flight and in the final phase turns on its active radar seeker to home on to the target.

Its warhead carries impact and proximity fuses so targets can be destroyed even if the missile does not score a direct hit.

Its radar system will be derived from that used in the French Mica air-to-air and Aster surface-to-air missiles. It will also be able to defeat advanced countermeasures.

At contract award in 2002, the then Defence Secretary, Geoff Hoon, said: 'Meteor is a new concept in air-to-air weaponry. Its unique air-breathing motor will make it very difficult to evade and state of the art electronics will make it the most effective air-to-air weapon we have seen.'

Meteor is made up of four sections: the radome enclosing the active radar; missile electronics and fuse system; the warhead and the ramjet rocket motor, all enclosed within a stealthy, low-drag, lightweight body. ■

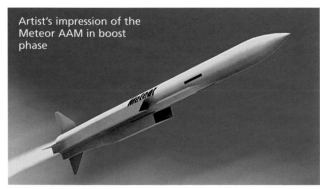

Artist's impression of the Meteor AAM in boost phase

Artist's impression of a Typhoon F2
launching a Meteor missile

The UK Military Flying Training System (UKMFTS) is a tri-Service programme with a multi-billion pound projected value over its 25-year life.

It is intended to provide a comprehensive military flying training system, catering for the needs of fast jet, multi-engine transport aircraft and helicopter pilots, weapon systems operators and rear crew for Royal Air Force, Royal Navy and Army Air Corps personnel.

This work is jointly led by the MoD central staff, who specify what MoD wants the programme to deliver, and the Defence Procurement Agency (DPA) UKMFTS project team, working in close collaboration with the three Services and Industry to provide the quality and quantity of training needed in the future.

UKMFTS will deliver all flying training up to the entry standard for the Operational Conversion Units (OCUs), or single–Service equivalents, which will retain responsibility for type-specific and operational role training.

In 2005, the DPA received bid proposals from the three competing consortia seeking to become the Training System Partner (TSP); Ascent (Lockheed Martin and the VT Group); Sterling (Thales Defence Ltd and The Boeing Company), and Vector (Kellogg Brown and Root Limited, EG&G/Lear Siegler Inc and Bombardier).

Bid receipt follows a detailed study phase undertaken between MoD and industry and marks the start of a period of detailed assessment and evaluation that will involve some 160 MoD subject matter experts and lead towards the intended identification of the preferred bidder during 2006.

The successful bidder will work closely with the MoD to incrementally replace military aircrew training across all three Services. The TSP will be responsible for managing the delivery of flying training, provision of some instructional manpower, the training management information system, facilities management, and procurement and support of some aircraft and Synthetic Training Equipment (STE).

The AJT function within UKMFTS will be provided by Hawk 128. In December 2004, a £158million contract was placed with the company for the design and development of the aircraft.

MoD is working closely with BAE Systems to manage the design of the avionics architecture, introduce a modern digital cockpit environment and deliver two trials aircraft to support the development and test flying.

Aircraft numbers, the delivery schedule and the date for Hawk 128's introduction to service are to be decided in due course.

UKMFTS is seeking to create a fully integrated and coherent training system working with industry to deliver this important programme. ∎

Jaguar pilots on a NATO detachment – future aircrew may be trained under the UKMFTS programme

A Tornado GR4 pilot in his cockpit – his
successors may be trained under UKMFTS

The Strategic Unmanned Air Vehicle (Experiment) project is run by a DPA project team of the same name, but is not a conventional project.

Its objective is to collect and evaluate the evidence which the MoD will use to decide whether strategic unmanned air vehicles (UAVs) can justify a place in future UK Armed Forces. If they do have a place, then follow-on acquisition projects will be launched to buy the equipment.

SUAV(E) and the associated project team were created in May 2005 following the refocusing of the old Future Offensive Air System (FOAS) programme into several work strands looking at systems and technologies that will support the MoD's deep strike capability in the medium to long term.

SUAV(E) manages the UAV aspects of this work. It will be collecting the evidence it needs from a number of existing and planned programmes both in the UK and beyond. The current plan is to produce sufficient evidence for well-founded decisions on Strategic UAVs to be made around the turn of the decade.

As part of its work, SUAV(E) runs a co-operative programme with the US's Joint Unmanned Combat Air System (J-UCAS) project office to determine the military benefit of uninhabited combat air systems for future coalition operations.

The SUAV(E) team, with support from the MoD central staff who specify the performance of future equipment, MoD's in-house research body, the defence scientific and technical laboratories and research agency QinetiQ, will work with US partners to develop appropriate coalition concepts of operations, assess interoperability issues and risks, and determine measures of effectiveness.

The programme was announced in 2005, and is due to complete in 2009.

Technology work continues in the UK with a number of companies, including BAE Systems. Other technology work is being taken forward as part of the European Technology Acquisition Programme, a menu of collaborative technology demonstrator programmes in which France, Germany, Italy, Spain, Sweden and the UK participate.

The team's work includes consideration of potential acquisition routes. At present, several routes, including international collaboration, remain possible.

Decisions will be taken in line with the Government's defence industrial policy, and in consultation with UK industry. ■

A Tornado GR4 strike aircraft pictured in the run-up to Operation Telic. The SUAV(E) project is looking at future deep strike technologies.

An image of a Raven UAV

The Future Strategic Tanker Aircraft (FSTA) service will replace the air-to-air refuelling capability and elements of the air transportation work undertaken by the RAF's current fleet of nineteen VC10 and nine TriStar aircraft. MoD is looking at a Private Finance Initiative solution which would provide a modern well-equipped fleet, while placing through-life risks of ownership with industry. The RAF would continue to retain responsibility for all military tasks, whilst the contractor would own, manage and maintain the aircraft and also provide training facilities and some personnel.

MoD will pay for the provision of the air-to-air refuelling and air transport (freight) capability on the basis of availability and usage, and payment will only be made when the service is delivered to a satisfactory standard. As the RAF will not need all of the aircraft for all of the time, the contractor will be able to earn extra revenue by using spare aircraft for commercial operations, earning Third Party Revenue, a key element of this PFI. However, the RAF would always

Artist's impressions of the FSTA refuelling two Typhoon F2s

have first call on all the aircraft in an emergency. The project has an estimated through-life cost of several billion pounds.

The MoD is in negotiation with AirTanker Ltd (ATr), a consortium specifically formed to deliver the FSTA service. The company combines the capabilities of its five shareholders: EADS, Rolls-Royce, Cobham, VT Group and Thales. ATr was announced as the MoD's Preferred Bidder for the FSTA PFI deal in February 2005.

Current plans envisage FSTA progressively entering into service early in the next decade (to ensure the full operational availability of the fleet over the next 27 years). ATr would be responsible for:

Acquisition of a fleet of new and used Airbus A330-200 aircraft: Commercial standard aircraft built and flight tested at Toulouse by Airbus. Wing manufacture at Bristol and Broughton (Airbus). Engine assembly at Derby (Rolls-Royce). Avionics & Mission systems at Raynes Park & Wells (Thales).

Aircraft conversion to tanker configuration, fitment of military avionics and certification: Aircraft conversion – Bournemouth (Cobham). Air Refuelling system – Wimborne (Cobham). Air certification – INTA (Instituto Nacional De Tecnica Aeroespacial) or Boscombe Down (QinetiQ).

Development of RAF Brize Norton, including extensive construction work, the provision of ground and air support equipment, ancillary vehicles, flight simulators (Crawley – Thales) and the installation of IT systems, and Provision of long term operational support, including crewing, training and maintenance (Logistic support – VT Group). ◼

Artist's image of FSTA trailing two refuelling drogues from underwing pods

Acurrent MoD study into Future Rotorcraft Capability, due to report by the end of 2006, is looking at how best to deliver our future rotorcraft lift requirement, particularly the balance between medium and large lift. It will look at the possibilities of both running on current aircraft and buying new.

The RAF-crewed Chinook heavy lift helicopter force forms part of the future rotorcraft capability in the guise of Chinook HC2/2A coherence and Chinook HC3 Fix to Field. The Chinook team is split between the HC2/2a element at Yeovilton and the HC3 element at DPA headquarters in Bristol.

Over the years the 40-strong Chinook fleet has received different equipment fits to fulfil varying operational roles. To enable more efficient fleet management, embodiment of future modifications (most significantly the Bowman communications system) and enable future support opportunities, a baseline specification is being established under the coherence programme.

A study last year recommended a Fix to Field solution as the probable best value for money solution to successfully bring a further eight Chinook HC3s into service. MoD is working with Boeing to ensure the proposed solution is mature and robust before taking the final decision on whether to proceed.

A Land Advanced Concept Phase (LACP) has also been approved and will look at how to best deliver MoD's future rotorcraft lift requirement, particularly the balance between medium and large helicopters. The RAF's Support Helicopter Force operates a fleet of 22 Merlin HC3 and 38 Puma medium lift helicopters along with the Chinook Force. A further 40 Sea King Mk4s/6c are operated by the Royal Navy in the

An RAF Puma in desert conditions – FRC is looking at a successor project

Commando role.

When these studies have been completed, the MoD will announce how it intends to take each programme forward.

Also under the FRC umbrella is a project to provide the Army and Royal Navy with a new light helicopter to succeed their existing combined fleet of some 170 Lynx helicopters.

MoD has announced that the AgustaWestland Future Lynx (FLynx) is the preferred procurement option to meet the Land Find and Maritime (Surface) Attack requirements of the FRC programme, subject to continuing successful negotiations with the company.

MoD has also agreed a Heads of Agreement with AgustaWestland which commits both sides to explore working together towards a long-term partnering and business transformation arrangement which is expected to provide significant improvements in efficiency and effectiveness in how MoD and the company support the helicopter fleet operated by the three Services. ∎

An RAF Chinook – improvements are under study as part of the FRC project

Search and Rescue Helicopter Programme

The Search and Rescue Helicopter Programme (SAR-H) is managed by a joint MoD/Maritime and Coastguard Agency (MCA) project team. The programme seeks to replace the search and rescue capability currently provided by the RAF and RN (using a mix of Sea King Mk3, 3a and 5 helicopters) and those provided by the MCA through a service contract.

Together, MoD and MCA provide a 24-hour military and civil SAR service for the UK SAR Region from 12 bases around the country, frequently assisted by RAF Nimrod maritime patrol aircraft and sometimes by RN vessels.

For over 60 years life-saving activities have been conducted in and around the UK, ranging from air/sea rescue hundreds of miles out into the Atlantic and mountain rescue, to recovering downed military aircrew on land and at sea.

MCA aircraft fly from bases at Stornoway, Sumborough, Lee-on-Solent and a daytime only base at Portland. RN aircraft fly from Naval Air Stations at Culdrose and Prestwick and RAF aircraft fly from air stations at Boulmer, Wattisham, Chivenor, Leconfield, Valley and Lossiemouth.

The existing SAR service is provided by 19 Sea King Mk3 and six Mk3a RAF aircraft, two of which normally deployed to the Falkland Islands. The RN SAR force is drawn from a fleet of about 15 Sea King Mk5s, of which approximately six are deployed on SAR duties.

The MoD/MCA project team was launched

A Sea King overhead

in January 2005 with the transfer of the project from what was the Support Amphibious Battlefield Rotorcraft (SABR) team. The project is investigating different ways of providing SAR capability and is exploring the potential for a combined MoD/MCA programme.

Possible options include joint or stand-alone MoD/MCA programmes, Public Private Partnership/Private Finance Initiative (PPP/PFI), conventional procurement or maintaining and running-on the current capability.

The results of this work will be used to inform parallel MOD and Department for Transport (DfT, the parent department of the MCA) business cases which will select the most appropriate procurement strategy.

Industry is being kept informed of the progress of this programme and industry consultation exercises have been carried out, involving helicopter manufacturers, operators and service providers.

The solution that emerges from the joint studies is planned to enter service in the early part of the next decade, initially with one operational base, before being extended to meet the full capability.

In the meantime, the MoD/MCA project team are also managing a competition to fill the capability at the four MCA sites, from 2007 to 2012, until the chosen solution is in place. ■

An RAF Search and Rescue helicopter from Chivenor   SAR H is looking at a successor service

Tactical Information Exchange Capability (TIEC)

The Royal Air Force and Royal Navy have a requirement for a modern tactical data link (TDL) capability that will enable the UK to participate more effectively in air operations – including those with allies.

To meet this requirement a project has been established within the Defence Procurement Agency Tactical Data Links team to study the best solution and plan for it to be fitted to the Tornado GR4/4A and Harrier GR9/9A aircraft, subject to MoD final approval.

The TIEC requirement is for the procurement of a capability that seamlessly, automatically and securely exchanges specified tactical information with national and coalition participants to improve aircrew situational awareness.

This means that Tornado and Harrier aircrew would be able to see the same networked tactical picture on their cockpit screens as other RAF and allied aircraft on a sortie. This picture would include location of friendly and hostile aircraft, ground targets and other information supplied through surveillance aircraft, such as the E3 Sentry.

Using this information, aircraft would be able to prosecute time sensitive targets more effectively, improve close air support of troops on the ground through exchange of information and imagery with other aircraft and increase their own ability to successfully complete missions.

TIEC also offers the promise of better combat identification, reducing the chance of friendly-fire engagements with both other aircraft and ground-based missile systems.

The TIEC requirements may be satisfied for each type of aircraft through data links using proven systems already fitted to some RAF aircraft, such as the Joint Tactical Information Distribution System/Link 16 and Variable Message Format-based messages exchanged using improved data modem technologies.

Assessment Phase studies now in progress will establish the optimum solution that can be provided and supported within programme affordability constraints.

Contractor BAE Systems and General Dynamics UK are working together on assessment phase studies that are expected to run through 2006.

Many RAF and RN aircraft, such as RAF E3 Sentries and Tornado F3 fighters and RN early warning Sea King helicopters are already fitted with data links to meet requirements for a networked air defence force.

The proposed TIEC project would extend this network of knowledge, data and imagery exchange throughout the RAF Tornado GR4 fleet and the joint RAF and RN-crewed Harrier GR9 fleet. ∎

RAF GR7s – the TIEC project is studying fitting successor GR9s with the latest networked data-links

A Tornado pilot – improvements to tactical information exchange are under study

SANS/JOANNA/DIRCM

Within the DPA Sensor Avionic and Navigation Systems and Air Electronic Warfare project team, there are several airborne radar technology demonstrator programmes in development. These programmes aim to demonstrate the enhanced performance and capabilities provided by Active Electronic Scanning Radar. Active Electronic Scanning benefits include improved identification, tracking and targeting of fast manoeuvrable air targets in a jamming environment, and air-to-ground day, night and all-weather targeting of strategic and mobile targets.

The flexibility of Active Electronic Scanning Radar will allow a single sensor to operate in multi-modes with a high degree of redundancy to support the enhanced capabilities required by current and future combat aircraft. These programmes are aimed at potentially providing an enhanced capability to both Typhoon and the Tornado GR4 depending on future requirements.

The team is running several

A DIRCM turret on a C-130

projects, both equipment acquisition and research, in the field of Electro-Optic Targeting. The main procurement programme is a targeting pod for Typhoon, enabling the aircraft to achieve a precision air-to-surface capability.

The pod chosen is the Litening III. This is a third-generation targeting pod that will greatly increase the performance currently provided by the existing in-service second-generation thermal imaging and laser designation (TIALD) pod.

The highlights are: longer stand-off ranges, greater image quality, higher reliability and reduced repair and maintenance times. Pods will be available for the Typhoon integration programme and 20 pods and associated support available to the Typhoon fleet in 2008.

Research is being carried out into technologies that are expected to feature in fourth generation targeting pods. In particular the Joint Airborne Navigation and Attack (JOANNA) project is investigating burst illumination laser imagery for target identification at increased ranges, and 2D-ATRICIA is developing algorithms for assist-ed target recognition/identification using imagery collected using platforms similar to JOANNA.

The Directed Infra Red Countermeasures (DIRCM) system provides a number of RAF, RM and AAC aircraft with a greatly improved protection against infra-red guided missiles including, in particular, shoulder-launched man-portable air defence systems.

As with some previous jammers, the DIRCM system uses modulated infra-red discharge lamps to defeat the missiles' guidance systems. However, the project team is procuring laser-based systems to improve DIRCM effectiveness, while at the same time reducing power consumption, weight and drag. These are now fitted to a number of transport aircraft. All future DIRCM systems are likely to use laser jamming sources. This will replace large DIRCM transmitters with the more compact small laser transmitter assemblies.

The project team is also developing a research package to investigate a new advanced concept of missile warning systems for use in the next generation of Defensive Aid Suites (DAS). ∎

Typhoon – technologies that could be used for future upgrades are under study

RAF Museum Hendon – new
Milestones of Flight Exhibition Hall

Combining the history of the RAF with a free, fun day out, the Royal Air Force Museum is Britain's only national museum dedicated wholly to aviation. With a world-class collection of aircraft, integrated with special exhibitions, films, interactives, artwork, engines, missiles, photographs, uniforms, medals and research and education facilities, the Royal Air Force Museum takes an innovative approach while keeping with tradition.

While offering a detailed insight into aviation technology, it also focuses on the people who made it possible – from daredevil early aviators, through wartime heroes, to the thousands of ordinary servicemen and women whose contribution shaped the world we live in today.

The Museum occupies two public sites at Hendon, London, and Cosford, Shropshire. Both tell the story of aviation with a unique brand of education and entertainment that make them a great free fun day out for all the family. Free parking and easy road and public transport access ensure they are easy to get to.

Situated in the West Midlands, Cosford is acknowledged as one of the top public attractions in the area, and is unique in that it includes both indoor and outdoor aircraft exhibits. The Cosford Visitor Centre, which includes a restaurant and souvenir shop, makes a perfect take-off point for a tour of the Museum site – including the wartime hangars in which many of the aircraft are housed, a

The beautifully restored Grahame-White Factory

number of them the only remaining examples in the world. The display includes over 80 aircraft along with one of the finest collections of missiles, rockets and engines in the world. Other features include the Michael Beetham Conservation Centre, the official British Airways Museum and a number of commercial passenger aircraft. Currently under construction is a stunning new exhibition hall which will tell the story of the Cold War. With Warsaw Pact and NATO aircraft as well as exhibits from the UK's three armed forces, the new development will

Milestones of Flight Exhibition

MBCC Meteor refurbishment

Iconic Spitfire wall display

set the scene from a social, political and military setting.

Cosford is on the A41, one mile south of junction 3 on the M54 and only 25 miles from Birmingham. It has its own railway station and visitors can also fly in on weekdays by prior permission.

The Royal Air Force Museum at Hendon is situated in north west London, just a few tube stops from the centre of the capital. Amongst the 100 aircraft is the chance to see some great film shows, artwork, medals and uniforms. The Battle of Britain Hall allows visitors to experience the dangerous days of 1940 when the country was under attack. With history sites and an awe-inspiring multi media show, visitors can feel a part of the events that shaped up to the Second World War.

New to Hendon is the Milestones of Flight exhibition – a stunning and dramatic display including suspended aircraft, time-wall, touch-screen plinths and split-level viewing. On the other hand the beautifully restored Grahame-White Factory is an example of an aircraft factory from the early days of British aviation. A historical building in its own right, it now contains classic aircraft of the time.

Museum facilities include a café, restaurant, outdoor arena and disabled access. Getting there is easy and the Museum is signposted from the A1, M1, A41, A5 and A406. The local tube is Colindale (Northern Line) and it is also close to Mill Hill Broadway (Thameslink Rail). The 303 bus stops right outside.

As well as all that, both Museums offer free entrance and a whole host of indoor and outdoor activities. ■

**Royal Air Force Museum,
Hendon,
Grahame Park Way,
London NW9 5LL**

020 8205 2266

**Royal Air Force Museum,
Cosford, Shifnal
Shropshire TF11 8UP**

**0870 606 2027
www.rafmuseum.org**

The mission of the Royal Air Force is to defend our national airspace and maintain the UK's role in the international arena. Overseas we bring aid and protection to the victims of disaster and war while at home we provide a lifeline to the many who count on us in times of emergency in our mountains and around our coastlines. To achieve all of our aims, we need people to join our team.

And we're not just Pilots. There are more than 60 careers in the RAF, from Engineering Technicians and Chefs to Doctors and Drivers – people to help us provide air power; gather intelligence, deliver troops and supplies to wherever they are needed around the world – and to support us while we're there.

We recruit people to join us both as full time regulars and as members of the Royal Auxiliary Air Force. We offer a lifestyle and experiences that you won't find anywhere else, together with great training opportunities, excellent salaries and a first class pension scheme.

Whatever your background, we'll help you maximise your potential. If you're up for the challenge the Royal Air Force can give you, read on to find out more.

www.rafcareers.com
www.rafreserves.com
Tel: 0845 605 5555

Anna Hooley
Weapon Systems Operator (Acoustic)

Sergeant Anna Hooley flies on a Nimrod squadron based at RAF Kinloss near Inverness. She was in her mid-twenties, and a member of the RAF Reserve, when she decided to pursue a full career in the regular Air Force.

'On a scheduled mission as a wet operator you can be doing anything from tracking a submarine with sonobuoys, to taking photographs at 200 feet with the window open, to being a lookout on a Search and Rescue mission. I really enjoy the fact that every individual in the crew can make a difference. Whoever finds a submarine can change the priority of the sortie – that goes for someone who's been in the crew for a few months right up to the most experienced member of the team.

'Wet' stations onboard a Nimrod MR2

'It's a great feeling when you detect a target. You've had extensive training – from basic military instruction to learning about submarines, sonobuoys and oceanography – all preparing you for the job. You feel like everything comes together.

'The best thing about it is that one day I can be told that I'm flying off to Puerto Rico or Brunei the next day. I've been out of the country for three months this year on different trips – although some of them were only exercises, several of them were operational.

'I love the crew atmosphere and the humour. There are 12 people on my team, with a real mix of experience. Crews tend to stay together for a long time so you all get to know each other's personalities and how best to work as a team. There's a lot of banter and we all get on well, whether it's 4 o'clock in the morning and we're getting ready to take off, or 11 o'clock at night and we're out on a Search and Rescue mission in the North Sea. If you can do a job that you enjoy, with a nice group of people, you've got it all.'

Ola 'Fash' Fashade
Engineer Officer (CE)

Flight Lieutenant Ola 'Fash' Fashade commands 'A' Flight of the Tactical Communications Wing (TCW), based at RAF Brize Norton in Oxfordshire. He was sponsored by the RAF while studying for his Electrical and Electronic Engineering degree at Brunel University.

'My first job was as a Flying Officer at RAF Bentley Priory in Middlesex. I was the only Engineer Officer on the station and reported directly to the station commander; that was really good. After that, I went back to Cranwell to do pre-employment training for this job.

'As TCW is a mobile unit, we

TCW setting up a tactical comms station

have to be able to survive and operate in locations as diverse as the Arctic and the Middle East. We're all aware that without communications you can't have air operations. My job is also about being a manager – about being a focal point for all kinds of problems, and representing my Flight to higher authority.

'I don't really go hands on and fix the kit myself but I have an overview of where the systems are. As Officer Commanding the Engineering Flight, I have 45 people working for me. They are all specialists on particular parts of the equipment, but not on the entire system. As I'm a trained systems engineer, I have the bigger picture and understand how they all fit together. If something isn't working, I need to identify the problem and determine which part of the whole system is causing it.

'On my Flight, the ultimate responsibility rests with me. Sorting out personnel issues has been very testing but it's all part of the leadership and management skills you learn on the Initial Officer Training course and during your professional engineering training.

'TCW has a very "can do" attitude. We travel a lot and basically just get out there and do the job, no matter what it is, where it is or how difficult it is. It's the biggest challenge I've ever had to face – but that's why I joined the RAF.'

Paul Millichamp
Regiment Gunner

Senior Aircraftman Paul Millichamp, from Birmingham, is a Gunner in the RAF Regiment. He gave up a civilian apprenticeship in building and joinery because he wanted to do something more exciting.

'My job is to patrol airfields overseas and make sure there aren't any threats. I'm also a para and have parachuted into hostile territory. Because we spend about four months of each year overseas, I've been to places and done things that most people will never experience – for example, I've worked in Sierra Leone in the jungle and in the desert in the Middle East. This job really opens your eyes to the rest of the world.

'It makes me really proud when I look back at what I've achieved. I've got a lot physically and mentally fitter since I joined the RAF. You don't have to be so fit when you first join – you work your way up to it, and if you've got what it takes, the RAF will give you all the training and help you need.

'In the evenings, I might play football, go to the gym or just head home – I live on base in families' accommodation with my wife. I also go out sometimes with my mates and have a few drinks. You work during the day and go out in the evenings with the same guys, so you build up a really strong friendship. That's what people mean by camaraderie.'

Airfield protection is a major role of Regiment Gunners

Louise Buttery
Musician

Nineteen-year-old Senior Aircraftwoman Louise Buttery from Stoke-on-Trent is a clarinettist in one of the RAF's bands. She joined the RAF a year ago to kick-start her career as a professional musician.

'I'm a member of loads of different ensembles. As well as the marching band, I play in a concert orchestra and a swing band, so there's plenty of variety. There's also quite a lot of travel: we play concerts in schools and for the public all around the UK; we're going to Cyprus to perform for the Queen's birthday celebrations and we'll spend almost a month doing rehearsals and shows at the Edinburgh tattoo.

'There's no such thing as an average day for an RAF musician. We often have either a rehearsal or a concert every day. But we do get a lot of free time – which people spend in the practice rooms or studying. Some people have already been to music college, so they're preparing for their Masters, while I'd like to do a degree and a Performance Diploma.

Clarinette ensemble on ceremonial duties

Careers: How to put yourself in the picture

For information on careers in the Royal Air Force, including detailed information on the current regulations, visit the RAF's website at **www.raf.mod.uk** or telephone **0845 605 5555**. Those who already wish to pursue the idea of a career in the RAF should contact their local Armed Forces Careers Office, listed under 'Armed Services' in the Yellow Pages, and ask to speak to an RAF Careers Adviser. ■

Aviation fuel replenishment – a vital task in aircraft support

'The training all starts when you join. At first you do military training, just like everyone in the RAF. Then you go on to learn the skills you need for the job. I had to learn how to march while playing my clarinet and do some extra music study. The training challenges you in every way that you can imagine. But you feel so good about yourself when you finish.'

There are more than 60 careers in the Royal Air Force and each one offers variety, excitement and the thrill of a challenge. And the RAF isn't just for pilots either – running a modern air force requires a vast team of specialists and support staff.

People such as technicians, chefs and suppliers; drivers, firefighters and gunners; dentists, doctors and nurses – and many, many more.

In choosing an RAF career, you will receive internationally recognised training, have the opportunity to gain professional qualifications and enjoy all the social opportunities that come with working in a young, dynamic environment. ■

The Ministry of Defence (MoD) is one of the largest, most progressive organisations in the country. A career with us provides a unique opportunity to work at the heart of UK Government, in an organisation that has international influence across the World.

The 70,000 civilians in MoD are employed to support the Armed Forces, including formulation of defence policy and advice to senior Military officers and Ministers.

The scope for people to find their vocation and develop personal and professional skills within an organisation of this size and complexity is unique. We are looking for people who can take the lead in any situation and who will build solid working relationships with others, whatever their discipline, background or culture. We need effective communicators, and people who can offer us their organisational skills, creativity and intellect.

In return, you'll find tremendous scope for personal and professional development, and high-quality, ongoing training opportunities (often leading to the achievement of a relevant professional qualification). We recognise talent, and provide more rapid development opportunities for the most talented.

We also offer flexible working patterns, a good maternity package and career break options. We consider equality of opportunity to be paramount, and are taking active steps to increase our representation of women, people from minority ethnic backgrounds and people

MoD Abbey Wood, near Bristol, is home to the Defence Procurement Agency

with disabilities – as they are currently under-represented throughout the Department.

MoD civilians are part of the wider Civil Service and, as such, are subject to the legal requirements governing Civil Service recruitment. All appointments must therefore be made on merit on the basis of fair and open competition. These values underpin our recruitment process.

Methods of Entry:
All MoD jobs are advertised on the MoD website at www.mod.uk, and in the national and local press.

Most of the posts are open to UK Nationals, Irish Nationals, Commonwealth Citizens, EEA Nationals and certain non-EEA family members. Check our website for details. ■

Glossary

AAR	Air-to-Air Refueling	CAP	Combat Air Patrol	JHC	Joint Helicopter Command
AAW	Anti-Air Warfare	CAS	Close Air Support	JRRF	Joint Rapid Reaction Force
ACCS	Air Command & Control System	CASOM	Conventionally Armed Stand-Off Missile	JSF	Joint Strike Fighter
ADGE	Air Defence Ground Environment			JTIDS	Joint Tactical Information Distribution System
AEROMED	Aeromedical Evacuation	CBU	Cluster Bomb Unit		
AEW	Airborne Early Warning	COMAO	Composite Air Operations	LGB	Laser Guided Bomb
AGM	Air-to-Ground Missile	CVF	Future Aircraft Carrier	LMG	Light Machine Gun
AIM-9L	Sidewinder SRAAM	DAS	Defensive Aids System	LTM	Laser Target Marker
ALARM	Air Launched Anti-Radiation Missile	DLO	Defence Logistics Organisation	MAD	Magnetic Anomaly Detector
		DPA	Defence Procurement Agency	MEDEVAC	Medical Evacuation
AMRAAM	Advanced Medium Range Air-to-Air Missile	DZ	Drop Zone	MR	Maritime Reconnaissance
		ECM	Electronic Counter Measures	MRA	Maritime Reconnaissance & Attack
ASACS	Airborne Surveillance and Control System	ELINT	Electronic Intelligence		
		ESM	Electronic Support Measures	MRT	Mountain Rescue Team
ASC	Air Surveillance & Control	EW	Electronic Warfare	MSC	Mission Support Cell
ASOC	Air Support Operations Centre	FAC	Forward Air Control	NATO	North Atlantic Treaty Organisation
ASRAAM	Advanced Short Range Air-to-Air Missile	FLIR	Forward Looking Infrared	NBC	Nuclear, Biological & Chemical
		GBAD	Ground Based Air Defence	NVG	Night-vision Goggles
ASTOR	Airborne Stand-Off Radar	GLO	Ground Liaison Officer	OAS	Offensive Air Support
ASW	Anti-Submarine Warfare	HAS	Hardened Aircraft Shelter	OCA	Offensive Counter Air
ATOC	Air Tactical Operations Centre	HF	High Frequency	ORBAT	Order of Battle
AWACS	Airborne Warning & Control System	HMI	Human-machine Interface	OSG	Offensive Support Group
		IFF	Identification Friend or Foe	PJHQ	Permanent Joint Headquarters
BMEWS	Ballistic Missile Early Warning System	IMINT	Imagery Intelligence	RAP	Recognised Air Picture
		IMSAT	Imagery Satellite	SAR	Search & Rescue
BVR	Beyond Visual Range	INAS	Inertial Navigation and Attack System	SATCOM	Satellite Communications
C2	Command and Control			SDR	Strategic Defence Review
C4I	Command, Control, Communications, Computers & Intelligence	IRF	Immediate Reaction Force	SH	Support Helicopter
		ISD	In Service Date	STOVL	Short Take-Off & Vertical Landing
		ISTAR	Intelligence, Surveillance, Target Acquisition & Reconnaissance	TACP	Tactical Air Control Party
CACS	Computer Assisted Command System			TIALD	Thermal Imaging Airborne Laser Designator
		JCA	Joint Combat Aircraft		
CAOC	Combined Air Operations Centre	JFH	Joint Force Harrier	UAV	Unmanned Aerial Vehicle

Squadron numbers by base and function

Air Combat – 1 Group

1(F) Sqn	RAF Cottesmore (Joint Force Harrier)	13 Harrier GR7/7A 1 Harrier GR9 1 Harrier T10
2(AC) Sqn	RAF Marham	12 Tornado GR4
3(F) Sqn	RAF Cottesmore (Joint Force Harrier)	13 Harrier GR7/7A 1 Harrier GR9 1 Harrier T10
4(AC) Sqn	RAF Cottesmore (Joint Force Harrier)	13 Harrier GR7/7A 2 Harrier GR9 1 Harrier T10
6 Sqn	RAF Coltishall	11 Jaguar GR3A 1 Jaguar T4
9(B)Sqn	RAF Marham	12 Tornado GR4
12(B) Sqn	RAF Lossiemouth	12 Tornado GR4
13 Sqn	RAF Marham	12 Tornado GR4
14 Sqn	RAF Lossiemouth	12 Tornado GR4
15(R) Sqn	RAF Lossiemouth	26 Tornado GR4
17(R) Sqn	RAF Coningsby	4 Typhoon F2 1 Typhoon T1
20(R) Sqn	RAF Wittering (Joint Force Harrier)	9 Harrier GR7/7A 5 Harrier T10
29(R) Sqn	RAF Coningsby	2 Typhoon F2 11 Typhoon T1
25(F) Sqn	RAF Leeming	16 Tornado F3
31 Sqn	RAF Marham	12 Tornado GR4
41(F) Sqn	RAF Coltishall	12 Jaguar GR3A 1 Jaguar T4
43(F) Sqn	RAF Leuchars	16 Tornado F3
56(R) Sqn	RAF Leuchars	20 Tornado F3
111(F) Sqn	RAF Leuchars	16 Tornado F3
617 Sqn	RAF Lossiemouth	12 Tornado GR4
1435 Flight	Falkland Islands	4 Tornado F3

100 Sqn	RAF Leeming	16 Hawk T1/1A
JFACTSU	RAF Leeming	2 Hawk T1/1A
(Joint Forward Air Control Training and Standards Unit)		

Air Combat Support – 2 Group

24 Sqn	RAF Lyneham (C-130J))	
30 Sqn	RAF Lyneham (C-130J))	49 C-130 C1/C3/C4/C5
47 Sqn	RAF Lyneham (C-130K))	
70 Sqn	RAF Lyneham (C-130K))	
99 Sqn	RAF Brize Norton	4 C-17
101 Sqn	RAF Brize Norton	16 VC10 C1K/K3/K4
216 Sqn	RAF Brize Norton	8 TriStar K1/KC1/C2/C2A
1312 Flight	Falkland Islands	1VC10 K3/K4 1 Hercules C1
32(Royal)Sqn	RAF Northolt	5 BAE 125 2 BAE 146 3 Twin Squirrel

Air Battle Management – 3 Group

8 Sqn	RAF Waddington	) 6 Sentry E-3D
23 Sqn	RAF Waddington	)
39 Sqn	RAF Marham	4 Canberra PR9
42(R) Sqn	RAF Kinloss	3 Nimrod MR2
51 Sqn	RAF Waddington	3 Nimrod R1
120 Sqn	RAF Kinloss	) 17 Nimrod MR2
201 Sqn	RAF Kinloss	)

JHC Support Helicopters

7 Sqn	RAF Odiham	7 Chinook HC2
18 Sqn	RAF Odiham	14 Chinook HC2
27 Sqn	RAF Odiham	9 Chinook HC2
28(AC) Sqn	RAF Benson	18 Merlin HC3
33 Sqn	RAF Benson	18 Puma HC1
78 Sqn	Falkland Islands	1 Chinook HC2
230 Sqn	RAF Aldergrove	13 Puma HC1

Search and Rescue

22 Squadron

A Flight	RMB Chivenor	)
B Flight	Wattisham	) 8 Sea King HAR3/3A
C Flight	RAF Valley	)

202 Squadron

A Flight	RAF Boulmer	)
D Flight	RAF Lossiemouth	) 8 Sea King HAR3/3A
E Flight	Leconfield	)

78 Sqn	Falkland Islands	2 Sea King HAR3
84 Sqn	RAF Akrotiri	4 Griffin HAR2
203(R) Sqn	RAF St Mawgan	3 Sea King HAR3/3A

FLYING TRAINING
Elementary
UAS/AEF/CFS (Univ. Air Sqns/Air Experience Flts/Central Flying School)

Various locations	94 Tutor

VGS (Volunteer Gliding Squadrons)

Various locations	84 Viking
	62 Vigilant

Basic

1 FTS	RAF Linton-on-Ouse	61 Tucano T1
3 FTS	RAF Cranwell	7 King Air 200
		9 Dominie T1
		4 Firefly T67

Advanced

DHFS	RAF Shawbury	25 Squirrel HT1
(Defence Helicopter Flying School)		7 Griffin HT1
4 FTS	RAF Valley	70 Hawk T1/1A
SARTU	RAF Valley	4 Griffin HT1
(SAR Training Unit)		

MISCELLANEOUS

RAFAT	RAF Scampton	10 Hawk T1A
(The Red Arrows)		
BBMF	RAF Coningsby	1 Lancaster B12
(Battle of Britain Memorial Flight)		2 Hurricane IIc
		3 Spitfire (Mk IIa, Vb, IXe)
		2 Spitfire MkXIX
		1 Dakota III
		2 Chipmunk T10
FJWOEU	RAF Coningsby	3 Tornado F3
(Fast-jet & Weapons		3 TornadoGR4
Operational Evaluation Unit)		1 JaguarGR3A
		3 Harrier GR9
		1 Harrier GR7
Station Flight	RAF Northolt	1 Islander CC2
RAFCAM	RAF Henlow	2 Hawk T1/1A
(Centre of Aviation Medicine)		(Based at Boscombe Down)

Note: Aircraft numbers reflect Required Operating Fleet

Index

Index